World Special Forces Insignia

(NOT INCLUDING BRITISH, UNITED STATES, WARSAW PACT, ISRAELI OR LEBANESE UNITS)

Text by GORDON ROTTMAN

Colour plates by SIMON McCOUAIG

OSPREY PUBLISHING LONDON

Published in 1989 by
Osprey Publishing Ltd
59 Grosvenor Street, London W1X 9DA
© Copyright 1989 Osprey Publishing Ltd

British Library Cataloguing in Publication Data
Rottman, Gordon L.
    World special forces insignia.—(Elite series)
    1. Special forces. Insignia
    I. Title   II. Series
    356.'16

    ISBN 0-85045-865-X

Filmset in Great Britain
Printed through Bookbuilders Ltd, Hong Kong

Author's Note

This book covers the special forces of over 50
countries; not included are those of Great Britain, the
U.S.A., the Warsaw Pact, Israel and Lebanon. Other
Osprey titles deal with these countries in far more
detail than space would here allow. Canada is
included under Western Europe, due to the wartime
mission of her relevant units.

Acknowledgements

A book covering such a large number of units and
countries could not have been possible without the
help of many. My appreciation is given to: Ken
Askins, Beryl Barnett, Ken Conboy, Antonio Carmo,
MSG Richard Dunlap, Mark Helber, Paul Lemmer,
Sgt. Torben Madsen, Ken Montgomery, Lt. Joakim
Paasikivi, Capt. J. R. P. Sererie, Shelby Stanton,
Nigel Thomas, Ron Volstad, Martin Windrow, US
Army OPFOR Training Det., and the many military
and naval attachés responding to my enquiries. A
very special thanks goes to the many members of the
Parachutists and Special Forces Insignia Collectors
who have so unselfishly contributed a vast amount of
otherwise unobtainable information over the years to
the *Chute and Dagger Newsletter*. Last, but not least, is
my appreciation for my wife Enriqueta, whose knack
for translating Spanish, French, Portuguese and
Italian was of invaluable use.

World Special Forces Insignia

Introduction

Roger Beaumont, in his *Military Elites*, questions whether élite forces are worth the cost and if their past effectiveness has enhanced overall force performance. His and others' works also address various adverse effects of the maintenance of élite units: 'leadership drain', the 'selection-destruction cycle', resource over-allocation, misutilisation, politically-backed origins, and resentment among conventional forces.

While all of these caveats are valid to certain degrees, many who critically appraise élite forces often miss the point entirely. Peacetime armies tend to be more tolerant of élite units, maintaining them as 'window dressing', either to make a political statement, an economic show of force, or to act as a pressure release for the young and daring. The romantic image and opportunities for challenge offered by élite forces do have a certain appeal to both image-conscious generals and enthusiastic 'firebrands'; but, today, the employment of such forces has increased in importance, as the nature of warfare evolves.

The Second World War fathered many of today's special forces, due to the need to buy time, to conserve forces (low investment/high return), to operate in restrictive terrain/climate environments, to experiment with new delivery methods and technology; and for political reasons. Political motivation and a revision of guerrilla warfare joined hands in the late 1950s and 1960s in two truly new forms of warfare: revolutionary insurgency, and international terrorism. These have permitted small, lightly-equipped political and ethnic minority groups to topple governments or achieve other political goals against larger and more sophisticated opposing

Commandos of 2 (Cdo.) Battalion, Belgian Para-Commando Regiment. They wear the Belgian camouflage jacket with olive trousers and the battalion's green beret: see Plate A1. The white dagger badge worn on the right shoulder in this photo seems to have been cut out of its green cloth patch leaving a narrow green edge. (Official)

forces. Counter-insurgency and counter-terrorist forces are a direct spin-off from these new forms of warfare—efforts, all too often unsuccessful, to defeat them.

Today's proliferation of special forces can be attributed to certain other definable considerations, e.g. restrictive terrain and climate. Examples abound of resources being expended to train and equip special units during World War II for terrain/climate-orientated operations. The British 52nd Div. was prepared to operate in Italy's mountains, only to fight on north-west Europe's plains; the US 71st Inf. Div., trained in Panama for Pacific island warfare, was subsequently deployed to central Europe—in the winter. Even though the US 10th Mountain Div., highly trained for that vertical environment, did fight in Italy, standard infantry divisions forced to operate there were actually as effective. But today's smaller armies, especially those of developing nations, demand maximum efficiency in force structure and employment. Mountain, jungle, arctic and desert areas require special purpose units trained, conditioned, and equipped to master these environ-ments. The pace at which conflicts develop today does not permit the luxury of the time needed to raise, develop, train, and condition conventional units for the rigours of combat in these extremes.

Specialised delivery means, or 'break-in' capability—i.e.

parachute, scuba/swimmer, helicopter, and amphibious landing—require specially trained and equipped units. While general purpose units can be trained to use the latter two means with equal effectiveness, specifically trained forces are maintained to perfect and advance these skills, as well as to spearhead the assault by trained general purpose units. During World War II, for example, the US Army conducted significantly more and vastly larger amphibious operations than the Marines; while in Vietnam, all infantry units conducted airmobile operations as effectively as the 1st Cavalry Div. (Airmobile).

Parachute insertion is the most controversial delivery means. Most opponents point out its high cost (although they should perhaps do a comparative cost analysis of equipping a mechanised infantry unit), and its lack of utility given the availability of the helicopter. Certainly parachute/airborne units should be trained in helicopter employment; but the 'chopper' has not completely replaced 'hitting the silk'. The option to deploy by parachute needs to be maintained, not only because the need might arise, but also for less tangible reasons. The concept of building *esprit de corps* by 'rites of passage'—acceptance by the 'tribe', common bonding between all ranks—for the purpose of unit cohesion, instilling aggressive-ness, and enhancing unit prestige, are lost on many

---

Abbreviations and Unit Designations

Units

Plt.	Platoon	Arty.	Artillery
Trp.	Troop	AT	Anti-Tank
Det.	Detachment	Cdo.	Commando
Co.	Company	CI	Counter-Insurgency
Sdn.	Squadron	CT	Counter-Terrorist
Bty.	Battery	Inf.	Infantry
Bn.	Battalion	LRRP	Long Range Recon Patrol
Regt.	Regiment	Para	Parachute (UK usage)
Gp.	Group	Pcht.	Parachute (US usage)
Bde.	Brigade	Recce.	Reconnaissance (UK)
Div.	Division	Recon	Reconnaissance (US)
Branch/Function		SAS	Special Air Service
Abn.	Airborne	SF	Special Forces
Ambl.	Airmobile	SOF	Special Operations Forces
Amph.	Amphibious	SPF	Special Purpose Forces

In Western European practice, and those countries influenced by them, units designated 'troops' are platoon-sized, 'squadrons' are company-sized, and 'regiments' are battalion-sized. Eastern European and US 'regiments' and 'groups' generally consist of several battalions. In Latin America the term 'group' has no fixed size indication, but is often battalion-sized. The term 'commando', besides identifying an organisation or member, also identifies a unit's size; *normally* of battalion-size. It is not uncommon for a unit to carry a designation indicating it is larger or smaller than it actually is, or its title may not give an indication to its size; its true size will follow its designation enclosed by parentheses. The term 'Jaeger', in its various spellings, literally translates as 'hunter' and designates units with a traditional title; originally identifying light infantry units with a scout or skirmisher rôle.

conventionally-minded soldiers. There is also one simple, often overlooked, benefit that makes parachute training worthwhile.

Everyone knows that tactical training is just that: despite all the lip-service paid to 'maximum realism allowed by peacetime training constraints', it is still training, even though training accidents do happen. But it is another matter to voluntarily and frequently throw oneself, with all sorts of paraphernalia strapped on, out of a perfectly good aircraft, in full knowledge of the risk of injury or even death. From the author's experience, riding a helicopter into a potentially 'hot' landing zone on active service is little different emotionally from waiting to make that vigorous exit over a Ft. Bragg drop zone. This pre-exposure to coping with combat stress and the control of fear makes parachute training well worth the effort in the interests of maintaining a peacetime immediate-action force capable of swift transition from the comforts of a modern garrison to the realities of combat half a world away, in a totally different climate, in what quite literally could be a matter of hours.

It is for these reasons that many nations maintain a parachute force, not because it is their principal means of delivery. The West Germans know that their 1 Air Landing Div., completely parachute-qualified, will probably never make a combat jump; its rôle is a helicopter-delivered anti-armour force; but they want troops who can face challenging odds with speed and flexibility, and sub-units capable of independent operations. Parachute delivery, in its 'normal' and more specialised modes (high altitude-low opening—HALO; high altitude-high opening—HAHO; and para-scuba) is of course critical as a means of clandestine insertion by many special operations forces.

Marines/naval infantry with much earlier origins, often with ties to naval coast artillery, are tasked with various rôles: ships' detachments, coastal defence, and navy base security, apart from service as a specialised assault landing force. Amphibious warfare has evolved into a sophisticated discipline involving specialised landing craft, amphibious assault vehicles, purpose-built support ships, helicopter operations, joint naval gunfire and air support, and complex cross-the-beach logistics.

The Cold War years saw the creation of various special operations forces intended to organise behind-the-lines guerrilla forces, and to execute small scale direct action operations and strategic reconnaissance missions. In the 1960s they further evolved into counter-insurgency advisors, i.e. training CI units in insurgency-prone developing nations, this form of warfare being pioneered by the USSF and the British SAS.

During this same period long range reconnaissance patrol (LRRP—a generic term) units began forming. Tasked with deep penetration *passive* intelligence collection missions, they are occasionally employed in other rôles.[1]

Ranger/commando-type units are generally considered as specialised light infantry, usually of battalion size, tasked with larger scale direct action and CI missions, often with an amphibious capability; they may or may not be parachute-qualified.

It must be remembered, however, that the designations given a nation's special forces units may be misleading as to its assigned rôle; e.g. the South Korean Special Forces have a ranger mission, and the New Zealand Ranger Sdn. had an SAS rôle.

Britain, France and the United States, the principal pioneers of special forces disciplines, have been extremely influential in the development of smaller nations' forces, not only in their training and methods of operation, but also in their uniforms, insignia, and traditions. Most developing nations' special forces received at least their initial training from visiting advisors and training teams, as well as attending courses in the supporting nations' military schools. Britain and France also offer such training through government-sponsored firms on a contractual basis using former military personnel, such as Defence Systems Ltd. and NAVFCO.

Selection of personnel differs vastly depending on a given unit's needs and national practices. With few exceptions, all personnel are volunteers, even though some nations accept conscripts, they must still volunteer for the duty. Mountain and jungle units usually seek inhabitants of those regions. High physical and mental standards, adaptability, initiative, motivation, security background, and political reliability are tested and evaluated by various means; this is followed by rigorous and realistic individual training emphasising self-reliance, as well as demanding mission-oriented unit training.

For the purposes of this book, special forces units are divided into two broad categories: special operations forces (SOFs) include SAS, SF, airborne ranger, commando, and LRRP units; special purpose forces (SPFs) are those units with more or less conventional organisation, though generally with lighter equipment. These include parachute/airborne infantry, airmobile/air assault, mountain, jungle, CI light infantry, and marine/naval infantry; and whether organised and equipped for a special means of delivery or to operate in restrictive terrain or climatic extremes, once on the ground, they generally fight as light infantry.

Not included in this work are units with a solely counter-terrorist mission, airborne civil police, air force security police and para-rescue units, naval scuba/swimmer units, and irregular or insurgent special units. Conspicuous by their absence are the special forces of Britain, the US, the Warsaw Pact, Israel, and Lebanon, all of which are well covered in other Osprey books[2]. This book's purpose is to provide an overview of the world's current special forces; no attempt is made to discuss all units of all nations.

The Beret: Symbol of the Elite

The beret, as an item of military headgear, has long been a symbol of special forces. Its recognition as such began in the early days of World War II, being ushered in by the British. In some armies, everyone wears a beret, but special forces are usually identified by unique colours. Additionally, they may be further identified by special beret badges, though some armies use a common one throughout.

The maroon beret, often referred to as 'red', has almost world-wide acceptance by the airborne community. It was officially adopted by the British Airborne Forces as a common identifying headgear by all subordinate units on 29 July 1942. Maroon was selected in late 1941 from a variety of colours offered; the choice was narrowed down to blue and maroon, and the latter supposedly chosen by Maj.Gen. F. A. M. 'Boy'

[2]See Elite 1, *The Paras: British Airborne Forces 1940–84*; MAA 156, *The Royal Marines 1956–84*; MAA 116, *The Special Air Service*; Elite 2, *The US Marine Corps since 1945*; Elite 4, *US Army Special Forces 1952–84*; Elite 13, *US Army Rangers and LRRP Units 1942–87*; Elite 5, *Soviet Bloc Elite Forces*; Elite 8, *Israeli Defence Forces since 1973*; Elite 18, *Israeli Elite Units since 1948*; MAA 165, *Armies in Lebanon 1982–84*; MAA 194, *Arab Armies of the Middle East Wars (2)*.

[1]Almost universally LRRPs employ small independently operating subunits referred to variously as patrols, teams, or troops.

Browning, OC Airborne Forces, as it was one of the colours used in his racing 'silks'.

The next colour to enter the scene was dark green. In mid-1940 the British Independent Companies requested identifiable headgear to promote *esprit de corps*. It was quickly decided that this would make the Commandos too conspicuous and create security problems; the request was turned down. The Dieppe raid again raised the issue and it was decided that unique headgear was appropriate. The green beret was introduced in the Special Service Bde. on 24 October 1942. Dropped in 1946, it was reintroduced by the Royal Marines when they assumed the commando rôle after the war. Its association with commandos led to its eventual adoption by similar units throughout the world, to include the USSF in 1961.

The British SAS unofficially adopted a sand-coloured beret in early 1942. In January 1944 it was officially replaced by the maroon, until the SAS were disbanded in October 1945. Reformed in 1947, the SAS retained the 'cherry beret' until July 1957 when the sand was re-adopted. This, too, is now used by many SAS-type units worldwide.

The black beret, principally identifiable with armoured forces in much of the world, is also recognised as the distinctive headgear of many ranger-type and CI infantry units, having been used unofficially by the US Army Rangers since 1951. Its use increased over the years, and on 20 December 1978 its wear by Ranger units was made official.

(There is one beret that pre-dates all of these: the blue Basque beret of the French *Chasseurs Alpins*, adopted in 1889 and still worn by French mountain troops.)

Of course many other colours of berets are used by the world's special forces, often related to past traditions. Other unique headgear is also proudly worn by some special forces, such as the West German *Bergmütze* and the Italian *Alpini* hat.

Western Europe

Western European SOFs are especially influenced by two of the region's militarily dominant nations, Britain and France. Their SOF traditions, insignia, and selection methods have served as the model for many SOFs in Europe and further afield. However, this is not to say that nations influenced by them have not followed their own SOF paths, developing unique traditions and building proud histories.

Belgium

Like so many other European nations, Belgium's SOFs had their beginnings with similar British forces. A Free Belgian para company was formed in 1942, serving under a number of titles until designated the Belgian SAS Regt. in 1945. Almost disbanded after the war, it was redesignated 1 Para Regt. SAS and subsequently Para Battalion. Jump training was conducted in Great Britain until the Belgian school opened at Schaffen in 1947.

The Cdo. Bn., tracing its origins to No. 10 (Inter-Allied) Cdo., was retained after the war, with a Cdo. School established at Marcé-Les-Dames. Both the Para and Cdo. Bns. provided volunteers for the *Bataillon Belge* serving in Korea in 1950–54. In 1952 the **Para-Cdo. Regt.** (*Le Régiment Para-Commando*) was formed at Namur, with the two battalions redesignated 1 Para and 2 Cdo. Battalions. Regardless of designation, both units were cross-trained, the Commandos having little trouble with the jump course, but the Paras having some difficulties with the rigours of the Commando course. A vigorous competitiveness between the units has been noted.

It was not long before companies from both battalions began rotating to the Congo. As troubles intensified 3 Para-Cdo. Bn., made up of both 1 and 2 Bn. members, was raised in 1956 and deployed to the Congo, and other units were sent as needed. The 4 Cdo. and 5 Para-Cdo. Bns. were formed in the Congo from reinforcement units sent from Belgium in 1959, while the 3rd was redesignated Para. The 6 Cdo. Bn. was formed there in 1960. The 11 and 13–16 Independent Cdo. Cos. also served in the Congo. Seven operational jumps were conducted during this period. The Congo was granted independence in late 1960 and all forces were returned to Belgium, except for 3 and 4 Bns., which moved to Ruanda-Urundi. The 5 and 6 Bns. were disbanded in Belgium. The 1 Bn. was again sent to Urundi in 1961, returning home with 3 Bn. in 1962; 4 Bn. was inactivated in Urundi and made a Reserve unit.

Further operations were conducted in the Congo (by now Zaire) in Nov. 1964, when hostage rescue missions were executed. The 1 Para Bn. and 12 Cdo. Co. jumped at Stanleyville, followed two days later by 11 and 13 Cdo. Cos. to release hostages at Paulis, both successful operations being dropped by US aircraft. In May 1978 1 and 3 Paras plus support elements returned to Zaire in support of the French Foreign Legion's 2 Para Regt. to rescue hostages at Kolwezi.

The mid-1970s saw the Para-Cdo. Regt. moved to Everberg, reorganised and assigned an interior defence rôle directly under the Army Staff. Elements are also committed to the NATO ACE-Allied Mobile Force[1]. The Regiment now has:

1 & 3 Para Bns.; 2 & 4 Cdo. Bns. (4th is Reserve); 31–39 Independent Cos.; Recce Sdn. (armoured car, co.-size); Arty. Bty. & AT Co.; Para & Cdo. Training Centres, School Co.; Medical Centre (deployable, co.-size); Frogman Det.; 1 ESR Company.

The 1 Special Recce Teams Co. (*1er Equipes Speciales de Reconnaissance Compagnie*) was formed in the early 1960s as a LRRP unit in support of I (Belgian) Corps. The 10 and 12 ESR Cos., assigned to 10 and 12 Mechanised Bdes. (Reserve), will provide LRRP support to 16 and 1 Divs. respectively upon mobilisation.

France

Europe's largest national airborne forces include a confusing array of SOFs and SPFs; and their lineage is no less bewildering, due to frequent changes of name and organisation during World War II, the Indochina War, 1946–54, and the Algerian War, 1954–62.

Pre-war company-sized units grew into parallel British- and US-sponsored **parachute infantry** battalions during 1943–45. The *1er Régiment de Chasseurs Parachutistes*, US-equipped, fought in NW Europe 1944–45; as did two 'assault' units, the *1er* and *3e Bataillons de Choc*. Two British-sponsored units had, in 1944–45, parallel identities as respectively 3 and 4 SAS, and 2e and 3e RCP. In India and Ceylon the British

---

[1]Allied Command Europe-Allied Mobile Force (Land)—ACE-AMF(L)—is an air transportable, brigade-sized, quick reaction force intended for employment on NATO's northern or southern flanks, formed in 1961. Component battalions and smaller units are provided by Belgium, Canada, Great Britain, Italy, Luxembourg, US, West Germany, and soon, Spain. Many of the units are parachute deliverable and must be initially self-supporting so as to ease the logistic burden.

Paratroopers of the French 11ᵉ Division Parachutiste board a C-160 transport. (Official)

supported the airborne 'SAS Bn. B', eventually absorbed in 1945 into the *5ᵉ Régiment d'Infanterie Coloniale*. After the French return to Indochina the build-up of airborne units for the war against the Vietminh was attended by many changes of title and 'paper' lineage and organisation, which need not concern us here.

Broadly, by the climactic period of the war in 1951–54, there was a floating force of some ten battalions in-country at any one time. They were made up of three types of unit: Metropolitan, Colonial, and Foreign. The '*paras Metros*' were French regulars (and, within France and Algeria, French conscripts) in RCPs and *Bataillons de Choc*. The '*paras Colos*' were volunteer regulars for service overseas; their titles changed most frequently, but by 1951 they were designated *Bataillons de Parachutistes Coloniaux*, BPCs. The Foreign Legion also fielded two *Bataillons Étrangers de Parachutistes*, BEPs. These units were very heavily engaged as quick-reaction reserves, fighting in all the major operations and making some 150 combat jumps.

Returning to France and N. Africa in 1954, the paratroopers were soon committed to the growing conflict in Algeria. In June 1956 the existing higher formations (25th Abn.Inf.Div. and Col.Pcht.Bde.) were reorganised into the 10th and 25th Pcht.Divs.:

10 Pcht.Div.
1ᵉʳ Régiment Étranger de Parachutistes (REP)
1ᵉʳ Régiment de Chasseurs Parachutistes (RCP)*
2ᵉ Régiment de Parachutistes Coloniaux (RPC)
3ᵉ RPC
6ᵉ RPC
13ᵉ Régiment de Dragons Parachutistes (RDP)
  plus divisional units,

An officer aspirant of France's 13ᵉ Régiment de Dragons Parachutistes photographed at Weisbaden, Federal Germany; rank is indicated by the single silver-lace (cavalry) bar worn horizontally on the chest patch, with two black transverse bars distinguishing it from the ranking of a sous-lieutenant. The olive tenue de combat mle 1964 is often retailored at unit level in élite units, to achieve a sharper appearance – here the jacket has been cut short and tightened at the waist. The enamelled regimental fob badge is pinned to the chest below the parachute brevet and name tab; and a bright blue shoulder strap slide (on the left) identifies the squadron. See Plate A3. (G-143 Inf.)

25 Pcht.Div.
2ᵉ REP
9ᵉ RCP*   (* = units transposed during 1960)
14ᵉ RCP
18ᵉ RCP
8ᵉ RPC
1ᵉʳ Régiment de Hussards Parachutistes (RHP)
  plus divisional units.

In December 1958 'Colonial' units were redesignated 'Marine', the RPCs becoming '*Régiments Parachutistes d'Infanterie de Marine*', RPIMa; note that in French usage this does not mean naval affiliation, the Marine units remaining part of the army.

The Algerian War saw the paras engaged, alongside the motorised units of the Foreign Legion, as the main mobile reserve; they reached a high level of proficiency, making very few combat jumps but pioneering the large-scale tactical use of helicopter insertion. This savage war of urban and wilderness guerrilla and counter-guerrilla operations was waged with great ruthlessness on both sides. Many paras identified with the white Algerian colonists; and when, in 1961, the intention of Gen. de Gaulle to agree to Algerian independence became

French beret badges ('*macarons*'). *Top left*: Troupes Aeroportées; silver; worn since 1948 by Metropolitan units; until 1958 by the Colonial parachute units; and from their formation in 1948 by the Foreign Legion parachute units. *Top right*: Marine Parachute Infantry, formerly Colonial Parachutists; silver winged hand and dagger, gold anchor; worn June 1958 to 1962, and from 1974 to present, with slight variations. *Bottom left*: Marine Parachute Infantry, 1962-74; all gold. *Bottom right*: Naval Fusilier Commandos; bronze; worn since May 1944. A similar pattern with the legend '1er B^{llon} F.M.COMMANDO' was worn 1943-44. (J. Gervasi and Ted Koppel)

clear, paratroopers of the 1er REP and 14^e and 18^e RCPs spearheaded a brief and almost bloodless putsch led by four retired generals. These units were disbanded following the collapse of the attempt, which did not attract the hoped-for support among the rest of the army. The two divisions were also disbanded, the remaining units being largely incorporated into the 11th Light Intervention Div.; this comprised 1er and 9^e RCP; 3^e, 6^e and 8^e RPIMa; 1er RHP; 13^e RDP; 35 Pcht. Arty., 17 Pcht.Engr., 14 Support & Sigs.Regts.; and 410 & 425 Support Battalions. In 1963 the last troops left Algeria; 11^e DLI relocated to southern France, taking in 2^e REP and — temporarily — the 9 Amph.Bde. of non-airborne Marine troops.

During this period French paras also served at Suez in 1956, making a combat jump and an amphibious landing; at Bizerta, Tunisia in 1961, making a combat jump; and in small numbers in other French colonies or associated territories in Africa. Since 1939 more than 6,000 paras have died in combat.

Redesignated in 1971, the division became *11^e Division Parachutiste*. Its units have since served in Djibouti, Chad, Zaire and Lebanon, and provide cadres for many ex-French colonies. It was the first formation assigned in 1983 to the new **Rapid Action Force**—FAR—headquartered at St. Germain-en-Laye, a multipurpose strike force to protect overseas interests

and to spearhead interior reaction forces. Supported by the 13,000-man logistics regiment 17^e RCS, its divisions are structured to meet specific threats, relying on various means of mobility, advanced weaponry, and high-tech. command and control systems. They include:

4 Ambl.Div., formed 1985 at Nancy. The 4^e DAM is a 6,400-man airmobile tank-killing formation, consisting of four anti-armour helicopter regiments (bns.) and 1 Inf.Regt., an ambl.bn. equipped with motorcycles, and light vehicles mounting AT weapons; a second infantry battalion is planned.

6 Lt.Armd.Div., formed 1984 at Nimes from 31 Armd. Division. The 7,500-man 6^e DLB can conduct recon., covering force, advance and rearguard missions with its two motorised infantry, two armoured car, and single artillery, engineer and support regts. (battalions).

9 Mne.Inf.Div., formed at St. Malo from the 11^e DP's 9 Amph.Bde., is an 8,100-man all-amphibious-trained formation comprising four motorised infantry, and single armoured car, artillery, engineer and support regts. (battalions).

11 Pcht.Div., now headquartered at Toulouse with 13,600 men in two brigades. Para infantry regiments, regardless of designation, are organised basically the same, with about 1,260 men in an HQ, recon. and support companies, and four rifle companies. *1 Bde.*: 3^e, 8^e RPIMa, 9^e RCP, 7^e RPCS (support regt.); *2 Bde.*: 1er RCP, 2^e REP, 6^e RPIMa, 14 RPCS; *Div. Troops*: 1er RPIMa, 11^e RHP (armd. car), 35 Para Arty.Regt., 17 Para Engr.Regt., 1er BPCS.

French Fusiliers-Marins Commandos, with slung FAMAS rifles, board a landing craft from a Zodiac inflatable boat. Swimming trunks are worn in conjunction with the field jacket when conducting waterborne operations. (Official)

Foreign legionnaires of France's Rapid Action Force man a Brandt 120mm rifled mortar during a deployment to Chad. (SERPA)

The 1ᵉʳ RPIMa and 2ᵉ REP serve in a commando rôle, receiving very specialised training. The 2ᵉ RPIMa, a non-divisional unit, has been headquartered on Réunion in the Indian Ocean since 1973 as a regional security force, and is also commando-trained. The 13ᵉ RDP, at Dieuze, with an element at Donauschingen, W. Germany, was formerly a motorised recon. unit like 1ᵉʳ RHP, but in the early 1960s was reorganised as a LRRP unit; directly under 1st French Army, it provides LRRP support for the entire French army (carrying the largest rucksacks this author has ever seen . . .).

Another FAR formation is the 9,100-strong *27 Alpine Div.* at Grenoble. The proud inheritor of the **Chasseurs Alpins** tradition stretching back to 1888, the 27ᵉ DA is organised into two half-brigades each of three units bearing traditional titles (which do not necessarily represent their actual current strength), *Bataillons de Chasseurs Alpins*, and *Régiments d'Infanterie Alpins*, BCA and RIA: 5ᵉ DB—6ᵉ, 7ᵉ & 13ᵉ BCA; 7ᵉ DB—11ᵉ &

27ᵉ BCA, 159ᵉ RIA. Divisional troops include armoured car, artillery, engineer and support regiments (bns.) plus a helicopter squadron.

The French army operates a number of regional and unit Commando Training Centres (CECdo) throughout France and its possessions, conducting four- and six-week courses.

The **Naval Rifle Commandos** (*Fusiliers-Marins Commandos*) are a French navy unit tracing their lineage to the original *1ᵉʳᵉ Compagnie de la Mer* of 1622, through many title changes. The *Fusiliers Marins* of 1856 were redesignated *Infanterie Coloniale* in the 1870s; a joint department within the War Ministry was established to oversee the Colonial Troops, which eventually came completely under the army's control, redesignated as *Troupes de Marine* in 1958.

Today's *Fusiliers-Marins Commandos* are direct descendants of the 1ère Cie. de FMC, French navy personnel retrained as infantry in Britain in 1941 and incorporated into No. 10 (Inter-Allied) Cdo. in 1942. In late 1943 the unit grew to *1er Bn. de FMC*, and in 1944 the battalion fought in Normandy attached to No. 4 Commando. Briefly disbanded after the war, the FMC were reconstituted in 1948, and fought, with varying strengths, in Indochina, Algeria, and at Suez; in Algeria they mustered three half-brigades.

Today, tasked with intervention and security missions, the *Groupement de Fusiliers-Marins Commandos* (GROUFUMACO) has some 579 men in six companies, all parachute qualified and some trained as combat swimmers. The *Commandement de Fusiliers-Marins* also oversees the FMC school, and 15 protection companies and sections which secure naval bases.

Netherlands

Small Dutch commando units were raised in 1942 as part of No. 10 (Inter-Allied) Cdo. and *Korps Insulinde* in the East Indies. Both were to form the basis of the Special Troops Regt. (*Regiment Speciale Troepen*) in the Dutch East Indies from 1946–50. Consisting of two para-commando type companies, the unit operated during the Indonesian revolt as part of the Royal Netherlands Indonesian Army (*Koninklijk Nederlands Indisch Leger*—KNIL) conducting several combat jumps.

After the Dutch withdrawal from Indonesia Special Troops personnel were consolidated with the Assault School (*Stormschool*) at Roosendaal to form the **Commando Troops Corps** (*Korps Commandotroepen*) on 1 July 1950. (The Assault School had been opened at Bloemendaal in 1945 to conduct commando training.) The Commandos did not undergo airborne training until 1963, which they received at the Belgian jump school until opening their own in 1966 at Gilze-Rijen. In 1964 the three-company Commando Corps, as part of a 'retrenchment' policy, was reduced to the 104 Observation and Recon. Co. (*104 Waarnemings-en Verkenningscompagnie*), a LRRP

Three different orders of dress worn by the Netherlands 104 Reconnaissance and Surveillance Company (see Plate B1). *Left to right*; olive drab field uniform with field cap, and Uzi SMG, as worn for LRRP missions; rigged with full jump equipment; and service dress – see Elite 16, *NATO Armies Today*, under Plate D, for general uniform practice. The green beret is worn with dark olive tunic, mid-tone trousers and light tan shirt and tie; a white lanyard and many qualification badges are worn here, including Federal German jump-wings on the right breast. (P.N.R.Thomas)

unit based at 's-Gravenhage and subordinate to I (Netherlands) Corps. Jump training is now conducted at Woensdrecht Air Base. The eight-week Elementary Commando Course is presented by the School Instruction Co., which also trains Marines and other military personnel; it also provides specialist courses and runs combat exercises for armoured infantry companies. The Staff and Staff Maintenance Co. provides school service support. Upon completing their active service, 104 Co. members are assigned to the reserve 305 Cdo. Troops Bn. (*305 Commandotroepenbataljon*), which has a wartime interior reaction force rôle.

The *Regiment de Marine* was formed in 1665, its successors serving in all wars in which the Dutch became involved, including with the KNIL in Indonesia and West New Guinea in the early 1960s. Today's **Royal Netherlands Marine Corps** (*Koninklijk Nederlands Korps Mariners*—KNKM), headquartered in Rotterdam, composed of 2,800 marines organised into a Corps Command, responsible for Corps HQ, operations and training; Home Command responsible for Netherlands' defence; and Antilles Command, for the defence of the Netherlands Antilles. The KNKM has a very close training and wartime contingency relationship with the British Royal Marines.

Units include 1 Amph. Combat Gp. (ACG) based at Doorm, along with the training establishments. It is a rapid deployment force principally aimed at operations in Norway, where it deploys once a year; while there, it is subordinate to 3 (UK) Cdo. Bde. RM, as it would be in wartime. Based on Curacao and Pinta Islands in the Netherlands Antilles, 2 ACG is responsible for that area's defence; and has the opportunity to conduct jungle training and joint exercises with other nations' marines in the Caribbean. Tasked principally with a home defence rôle, 3 ACG is a reserve unit (not counted in total strength) to which marines completing their active service are assigned. The ACG consists of 700 marines in an HQ, service support, combat support, and three rifle companies. 'Whisky' Co., a separate parachute-trained unit similar to the British RM Mountain and Arctic Warfare Cadre, trains extensively with 45 Cdo. RM in Norway and again is under its wartime operational control. Co. Boat Gp. is an assault craft unit specially trained in arctic operations and aligned with 539

Royal Netherlands Marines of the 1st Amphibious Combat Group brace each other while fording a stream in Norway, their designated area of operations in wartime. They wear British DPM field jackets and olive trousers; see Plate B2. (Official)

Paratroopers of the Federal German army rappel from a UH-1D helicopter wearing full equipment and packs. Though jump-trained, their mission is largely as heli-borne troops. (Official)

Assault Sdn. RM, which also supports 3 Cdo. Bde. RM. The final unit is 7 Special Boat Section, made up of divers, combat swimmers and canoeists in the same manner as its RM SBS counterpart: its base is aboard KNS *Thetis*.

West Germany

Having fielded 14 *Fallschirmjäger* divisions in World War II, the newly formed *Bundeswehr* was not initially permitted an airborne unit, as it was judged that such a unit was offensive in nature and that the West German Army was a purely defensive force. In 1956 approval was given, and the cadre for a jump school began training under the US 11th Abn. Div.; at the end of the year an air landing brigade was formed at Altenstadt-Schögau, along with the school. In January 1957 the brigade was expanded to form **1 Air Landing Div.** (*1. Luftlanddivision*—1. LL Div.) and moved to Esslingen, consisting at that time of only 25. LL Bde. and some divisional troops. It was another year before subordinate units were fully formed and the division finally committed to NATO. The 26. LL Bde. and a reserve brigade were raised in 1959, along with a separate battalion attached to 5. *Panzerdivision*; in 1970 this battalion formed the basis for 27. LL Bde., to bring the division to full strength. Later the reserve brigade was disbanded and its battalions assigned to the active brigades.

The Division is a controlling headquarters for the three brigades, each of which is attached to a corps, providing them with an airborne/airmobile anti-armour reserve force:

1. LL Div. HQ—Bruschal
25. LL Bde.—Schwarswald, II Corps
26. LL Bde.—Saarlouis, III Corps
27. LL Bde.—Lippstadt, I Corps

Each brigade has four air landing battalions (one is reserve) and HQ, supply, medical, AT, mortar, and engineer companies totalling about 2,800 *Fallschirmtruppen*. A battalion has an HQ and supply, two light infantry (*Jägerkompanien*), and two AT companies (*Pänzerjägerkompanien*). Battalions are designated by their parent brigade's number followed by 1-3 (0 for reserve bn.), e.g. Bn. 262 (additionally tasked to ACE-AMF) is the second battalion of 26. LL Brigade. This will all change in 1989 when the testing of Army Structure 2000 begins. Two airmobile (*luftbewegliche*) divisions will be formed, each with an existing air landing brigade, new anti-armour helicopter brigade, and the existing corps aviation battalion, and assigned to I and II Corps. Two new Dutch airmobile battalions may be incorporated into I Corps' division. III Corps will have only a mixed *luftbeweglichebrigade*.

Paratroop volunteers, most from among conscripts, receive basic training in battalions/companies and then attend the Air Landing and Air Transport School (*Luftland und Luftransport Schule*) at Altenstadt. The new *Fallschirmjäger* return to their units for advanced combat training, which includes the Close Combatant (*Einzelkampfer*) and Hunter Combat (*Jägerkampf*) courses.

The Long-Range Scout Troops (*Fernspähtruppen*) were formed in the early 1960s under the NATO LRRP concept. Each of the 200-man long-range scout companies (*Fernspähkompanie*—Fsk.) supports a corps, but they are not integral parts of an LL brigade, as is often reported:

Fsk. 100—Braunschweig, I Corps
Fsk. 200—Weingarten, II Corps
Fsk. 300—Fitslar, III Corps

Fernspähtruppen are trained by the German National Wing (II Wing) of NATO's International LRRP School[1] in Weingarten. II Wing was formed as Long-Range Scout Training Centre 900 in 1979 and its name changed the following year. Another unit is the Long-Range Evaluation Co. (*Fernspäh-hauswertekompanie*), a signal unit at Weingarten, which links all three companies' signal platoons with the Army Staff.

The **Mountain Troops** (*Gebirgstruppen*) have a long and proud history, the first such units being formed in 1781 by Bavaria. The *Gebirgsjäger* were used extensively in both World Wars. The *1 Gebirgsdivision*, headquartered at Garmisch-Partenkirchen, was formed in the mid-1950s as a 'pure' *Gebirgstruppen* formation. Over the years, however, its subordinate brigades have gradually been converted to mechanised units, so that now only *23. Gebirgsjägerbrigade* is organised and equipped to operate in the traditional alpine manner. The other brigades are *22. Panzergrenadier* and *24. Panzer*. The *23. Geb.Jäg.Bde.*, based at Bad Reichenhall, consists of *231–234 Geb.Jäg.* and 235 Arty.Bns. plus HQ, AT, engineer, supply, NBC, and mule-transport companies (all designated 230). The brigade is extensively trained in light infantry, anti-armour, mountain warfare, and cross-country skiing. Selected personnel undertake the rigorous Army Mountain Leader (*Heeresbergführer*) course, which qualifies them as guides and instructors.

Switzerland

Preparations began in 1967 for the creation of a LRRP unit in the Swiss Army. Formed in 1970 as *Fallschirm-Grenadier-Kompanie 17*, it was placed under the control of the air force, an integral part of the army. It was later redesignated Long-Range Scout Co. 17 (*Fernspäh-Kompanie*). Those trying out as *Fernspäher* candidates begin at age 17, with 500–700 applying annually through the Swiss Aero Club; about 300 pass the screening and educational requirements, and of these only about 80 pass the physical and psychological exam at the Air Force Medical Centre. At age 18 these men return for static-line and freefall parachute training, with about half meeting the course requirements. These return at age 19 for Freefall Course 2 which about 30 pass each year. At age 20 those still wishing to become a *Fernspäher* receive further screening and testing at the AF Medical Centre. In this way about 20 recruits are permitted to join the unit each year where they complete a 21-week *Fernspäh* school. The 100 members of the unit (roughly equal numbers of officers, NCOs and soldiers) are actually 'reservists' in the Swiss sense, and keep their uniforms and equipment (including parachutes, weapon and ammunition) at home. They conduct exercises and jumps for at least five weeks a year to maintain their tactical, HALO, and mountain parachuting skills. Most are retained in the unit until the age of 33.

Canada

The 1st Canadian Para Bn. was formed on 1 July 1942 and subsequently served with the British 6th Abn. Div. in Europe. The 2nd CPB (later 1st Canadian Special Service Bn.) was formed on 16 July as an administrative organisation for personnel assigned to the joint US/Canadian 1st Special

A *Fernspäher* of the Swiss Long Range Reconnaissance Company 17 practises ice-climbing skills; he is armed with a SIG SG510 rifle. (Official)

Service Force[2]. Post-war parachute units were not formed until 1948 when the Mobile Striking Force was established, composed of three, two-battalion (three during the Korean War) regiments; Princess Patricia's Canadian Light Inf. (PPCLI), Royal Canadian Regt. (RCR), and *Royal 22ᵉ Régiment* (R22R, French-speaking), one of each regiment's battalions being parachute qualified, a privilege they switched every two years. All MSF battalions served in Korea as part of the Commonwealth Div's. 25th Canadian Inf.Bde.Gp., though no jumps were made. In 1958 the rotation of parachute duties ceased, and each regiment contributed only a permanent parachute company group. On 8 April 1968 the **Canadian Abn. Regt.** was formed, consisting of 2 Abn. Cdo. (PPCLI), 1 Abn. Bty. (Royal Canadian Arty.), 1 Abn. Field Sdn. (engineers) at Edmonton; and 1 Abn. Cdo. (R22R) at Valcartier.

On 1 April 1977 the 1st Special Service Force was established as a 3,500-man brigade-sized reaction force at Canadian Forces Base Petawawa, and is composed of:

Canadian Abn. Regt.: *1ᵉ Cdo. Aeroporté* (R22R), 2nd Abn.Cdo. (PPCLI), 3rd Abn.Cdo. (RCR); 1st Bn. RCR (motorised inf.); Royal Canadian Dragoons (armoured recce sdn.); 2nd Regt. Royal Canadian Horse Arty. (bn.); 2nd Combat Engr. Regt. (bn.); 2nd Service Bn.; 427th Tactical Helicopter Squadron.

The airborne commandos are company-sized, with 150 troops each. The CAR is the only airborne unit, but the others have company- or platoon-sized subunits. The Canadian Abn. Centre (jump school) is also located at Petawawa.

---

[1] ILRRPS is a joint effort, formed in 1979, supported by the UK, West Germany, Belgium, and to a lesser extent, other NATO nations. LRRPs and other SOFs from all NATO forces undertake the many excellent courses offered.

[2] See First Special Service Force 1942–44, *Military Illustrated Past & Present* Nos. 1 & 2, 1986.

Northern Europe

While Denmark and Norway have been influenced by British SOFs, Finland and Sweden have taken a different track while maintaining their early military traditions.

Denmark

The first Jaeger Corps of two battalions was formed in 1785 and used for reconnaissance, often employing small boats. In peacetime they served as woodsmen in the king's forests, or as government clerks—which says something of their quality. They were volunteers, as are today's Jaegers, and had to be 'good looking', most certainly not a requirement for today's recruits. Around the turn of the century the Jaegers became standard infantry battalions.

Today's *Jaegerkorpset* was formed on 1 November 1961 as a

Two Canadian jump-masters of the 1st Special Service Force – note shoulder patches – inspect men of the US 82nd Airborne Division before a jump. Both wear maroon berets and British DPM smocks. From their subdued shoulder titles, the kneeling man is from the parachute element of the 1st Horse Artillery, the standing man from that of 2nd Combat Engineer Regiment. See Plate B6. (Official)

LRRP unit along SAS lines. They attended the German jump school until opening their own in 1964. Volunteers are accepted from the army, navy and air force after serving at least a year. They first undertake the eight-week Patrol Course (*Patruljeuvrus*), also attended by recon. unit members, but for potential Jaegers it is known as Selection 1. Those few making it then endure an eight-week Selection 2, followed by a scout swimmer course run by the navy's Frogman Corps (*Froemandskorpset*—the only other airborne unit), parachute, freefall (HALO and HAHO), and speciality courses. They are then on probation for a year. It is not unusual for only one or two men to be selected per year—at one point an officer had not made it for five years! The reason for this is that a certain personality profile and attitude are looked for. The company-sized unit, subordinate only to the Chief of Defence, is secretive about its operational capabilities and will only reveal that it is composed of an HQ, training platoon (which runs the Patrolling, Selection and jump courses), maintenance and signal elements, and a number of patrols (plus some reserve patrols). From the author's experience, this is a highly skilled and flexible unit, a key requisite for LRRPs.

Finland

While Finland established a jump school in 1961, its cadre trained by the Swedes, there is no permanent airborne unit. Selected conscripts spend their entire eleven months of active duty at the Airborne Jaeger School (*Laskuvarjojääkärikoulu*—

LJK) at Utti undergoing parachute, ranger-type, and speciality training. In wartime they would be assigned to SPF units such as the Lapland Inf.Bn. at Sodankya and the independent Sissi (*Sisscjä*) battalions. Sissi translates as 'partisan' and is the equivalent of jaegers—light infantry ski units which proved to be extremely effective against the Soviets during the 1939–40 Winter War. The Finns do have units designated jaeger, first trained by the Germans in 1915, but since 1981 they are anti-armour trained light infantry assigned to jaeger brigades (*Jääkäniprikaati*—JPr).

One jaeger unit, however, does have an SOF rôle. The

A lieutenant of Sweden's Northlands Dragoon Regiment demonstrates an FFV anti-personnel mine, the Swedish equivalent of the Claymore. He wears the dark olive m/59 uniform; light drab collar patches edged with light olive drab; and the 'JÄGARE' title in gold and black – see Plate C4b.. (J.Paasikivi)

A Swedish *Jägare* during 1987 troop trials of the new m/90 camouflage uniform system, in a splinter pattern of black, mid-olive and pale green-drab. The assault rifle is the new AK-5. (J.Paasikivi)

Coastal Jaeger Bn. (*Rannikojääkänpataljoona*—RannJP) was formed in 1952 as the Coastal Inf.Bn. of 1st Coast Arty. Regiment. Redesignated and made separate in 1960, it is based on the coast south-west of Helsinki. It is tasked with ranger-type operations involving coast defence, reconnaissance, and small direct action missions. The 'marine commandos', as they are often called, operate their own school which includes small craft handling and raids on occupied islands. Some personnel attend the LJK as well.

Norway

Two small commando-type units were formed with British assistance in World War II, but it was not until May 1962 that a jump school was established at Trandum. No airborne units as such exist, with the exception of the *Jeger* Plt. of Bde. North (*Brigaden i Nord*) located at Heggelia, and another in support of the frontier battalions in the Finnmark area. The jump school, referred to as the Jaeger School (*Jegerkole*), conducts both parachute and scout training for recon. units. Some Home Guard (*Heimevernet*) members are attached to the British 45 Cdo. RM when it trains in Norway and have undertaken commando training.

The Norwegian Navy has two Naval Jaeger Companies at Ramsund Navy Station. They operate their own school

specialising in combat swimming, scuba, small boat handling, demolitions, reconnaissance, close combat, and basic climbing. After 16 weeks of training the ten or so graduates attend the *Jegerkole* to become parachute qualified.

Sweden

Like Finland, Sweden has no permanently established airborne units, but does have a jump school that also conducts ranger-type training. The Army Parachute-Jaeger School (*Arméns fallskarmsjägerkola*—FJS) was established in 1952 at Karlsborg. Each year about 200 conscripts attend the school and within the first month are reduced to 60–100. The course begins in June, but in the winter is moved to Boden for arctic training for the remainder of its ten month duration, which includes survival, reconnaissance, raid, ambush, and close combat training. Some graduates are selected for NCO and officer training. But they, like the enlisted men, are discharged into the reserves and assigned 'on paper' to regiments. They do have 'War-Placing Orders' that would put most in independent ranger-type platoons to conduct wartime scouting and small scale raid missions in support of brigades.

In 1910 the Norrbotten Regt. (Inf. 19 or *I19*) formed a new unit which came to be known as the 'Skiers Battalion'. In 1942 it was redesignated I19K and moved to Kiruna. Trained in northern forest and arctic combat, it was re-formed in 1945 as the Forest Jaeger School (*Fältjägarekola*), later simply Jaeger School, remaining in the same location. In 1975 the School and Kiruna Defence Area staff provided the assets to form Lapland Jaeger Regt. (Inf. 22)—*Lapplands jägaregmente (I22)*. I22 has two missions: training and war planning. Each year over 500

An exhausted squad of Swedish Coastal Jaegers return from a patrol exercise aboard one of the unit's sea transport craft; their weapons are G3 assault rifles and MAG machine guns. The man second left can be seen to wear the unit's green beret and trident badge – see Plate C6. (Official)

Swedish beret badges, all in gold colour; badge model numbers quoted. *Left to right*: **Life Hussar Regiment, K3 (m/78); Lapland Jaeger Regiment, I22 (m/60); Northlands Dragoon Regiment, K4 (m/60); Army Parachute-Jaeger School (m/53-60).** (Official)

conscripts are trained by I22, about 350 as Jaegers and the rest as support personnel. Upon release from active service they are given war-placing orders for I22's numerous independent border jaeger and divisional recon. companies, tasked with a LRRP rôle. Each year I22 also conducts refresher training for 1,500–3,000 reservists plus exercises for officers.

The other two jaeger units have similar missions, but trace cavalry lineage. The Life Hussars Regt. (Cav. 3)—*Livregemente husarer (K3)*—at Karlsborg, co-located with the FJS, trains divisional recon. companies for use in central and southern Sweden. The Northlands Dragoons Regt. (Cav. 4)—*Norrlands dragonerregemente (K4)*—at Arvidsjaur trains independent arctic jaeger battalions for use in northern Sweden.

The Coastal Jaegers (*Kustjägare*), referred to as 'amphibious rangers', are a navy unit subordinate to Waxholm Coast Arty. Regt. 1. Like the army jaegers, they are made up of conscripts who undertake a ten month course and are then released into the reserves with war-placing orders. Wartime assignments are to numerous 'combat swimmer canoeist companies', two of which are airborne qualified. Their missions are similar to those of their Finnish counterparts. There are also diver and support units. The Swedes are very secretive about the various jaeger units' wartime deployments, not revealing the number of subordinate units each regiment will raise.

Southern Europe

This region's SOF organisations are heavily influenced by their countries' rugged terrain, proximity to the sea, and, in most cases, their local guerrilla warfare traditions.

Italy

Italy's first **parachute** unit was formed in 1938 in Libya. Expansion was rapid, and by 1941 there were no less than nine battalions in the army alone, the other services also forming units. More battalions were formed in 1942, along with parachute artillery and combat support units. To command the many units, regiments began forming in 1939 and subsequently the 185th Para Div. *'Folgore'*—'Lightning'—was established in 1942. In 1943 the 184th Para Div. *Nembo* was formed, and plans were made for another. With the September armistice, Italian airborne forces, like the rest of the armed forces, split into two camps; the German-controlled Socialists and the Allied-aligned Monarchists. Both sides raised new parachute units using the same pre-armistice titles, leading to some confusion. Few combat jumps were made by the Italians,

most being executed by X Assault Regt. *'Arditi'*, a commando-type unit raised in 1942.

Post-war Italy established a parachute school in Rome in 1947, moving it to Viterbo in 1949. The Para Bn. of the Ground Corps was formed in 1948 followed by a roster of specialised units: 1st Gp. Para Tactical, 1951 (reinforced bn.); Alpine Para Plts., 1952 (five formed); 1st Bn. Para *Carabinieri*, 1954[1]; Para Saboteur Bn., 1955 (raiders); and Para Arty. Bty., 1959 (later a battalion).

The School of Military Parachuting (*Scuòla Militare de Paracadutismo*), after several name changes, was moved to its present location at Pisa in 1958. The 1st Para Regt. was created in 1962 to control most of these units. Expanded to a Para Bde. in 1963, additional parachute battalions (*Battaglione Paracadutisti*) were added over the years. In 1962 the Objective Acquisition Gp. (*Gruppo Acquisizione Obiettivi*) was formed, a small LRRP unit for locating behind-the-lines targets for the 3rd Missile Bde. (initially with Honest John, now Lance equipped); it is now designated 13th GAO. In 1967 the Para Bde. was redesignated *Brigata Paracadutisti 'Folgore'*. Based at Leghorn, the World War II SOF centre, it now consists of:

HQ, Para Command & Service Co. 'Folgore'	Para AT Co. 'Folgore'
1st Bn. Para *Carabinieri* 'Tuscania'	Para Engineer Co. 'Folgore'
2nd Bn. Para 'Tarquinia'	Para Signals Co. 'Folgore'
3rd Bn. Para 'Poggio Rusco'	Para Aerial Resupply Co. 'Folgore'
5th Bn. Para 'El Alamein'	
9th Bn. Para Raider 'Col. Moschin'	Para *Carabinieri* Maintenance Co. 'Folgore'
185th Gp. Para Arty. 'Viterbo' (bn.)	Para Logistics Bn. 'Folgore'
	26th Helicopter Sdn. Gp.

The 9th Bn. Para Raider (*Incursore*) was formed from the original 9th Bn. Para Saboteur (*Sabotatore*) in the early 1980s. The five alpine brigades each have a para platoon trained in advanced climbing, ski, and reconnaissance skills. IV Alpine Corps also has IV Co. Alpine Para with the same capabilities. There is also an Airborne Troops Medical Centre. The Para Recon. Co. (*Compagnia Esploratori Paracadutisti*) appears to have been disbanded.

The **Alpine** troops (*Alpini*) were formed prior to the turn of the century. Serving with distinction in all of Italy's wars, e.g. six divisions in World War II, they have always recruited from the northern mountain regions, a concept still practised. The conscripts undertake three months' initial training in the 2nd Alpine Regt., completing their 12 months' active duty in one of the brigades where they learn the required mountain and speciality skills. Released into the reserves, they can report to their pre-designated units rapidly since they live nearby. The five *Brigata Alpini* are the 'Cadore', 'Julia', 'Orobica', 'Taurinese',

---

[1]The *Carabinieri* (Carabiniers) are the senior branch of the army. They perform military and national police, counter-intelligence, and other special security duties.

and '*Tridentia*', each composed of: three or five infantry and two artillery battalions (two also have a defence bn.); motorised infantry, engineer and signal companies; para and *Carabinieri* platoons; and a logistics regiment, all trained and equipped for the demands of high alpine warfare. All battalions are named after local mountains and smaller units carry the brigade's title. The brigades, and numerous corps troops, are under the command of IV Alpine Corps headquartered at Bolzano, whose sector covers the entire northern frontier.

The army's *Lagunari* were originally formed as 'amphibious engineers' prior to the turn of the century, operating in the vicinity of Venice. Re-established in 1951 as **amphibious infantry**, they were stationed on the northern Adriatic Sea coast. Today they consist of one each infantry and support battalions based at Venice. The best known Italian amphibious troops are the navy's 'San Marcos'. Originating from the World War I Naval Bde. (*Brigata Marina*), the organisation received the name of Venice's patron saint for its valiant defence of the city. Redesignated *Marina Reggimento 'San Marco'* in 1919, it was reduced to a battalion that same year. A special unit of the battalion was sent to Shanhaikwan, China, in 1924 where it remained until interned by the Japanese in 1943. The 'San Marcos' remaining in Italy were to fight in Ethiopia, Albania, North Africa, and on the Italian mainland. Increased to a regiment on the eve of World War II, it was to grow to

Wearing special camouflage overalls, members of the Greek Special Raider Force Battalion, Para-Commando Division collect up their equipment after a cliff assault exercise on an Aegean island. (Official)

seven battalions, one of which was parachute trained (1941). Both Socialist and Monarchist forces were to form units designated 'San Marco' after the armistice. The British-sponsored three-battalion regiment was inactivated after the war. The 'San Marcos' were reactivated on 1 January 1965 as *Marina Battaglione 'San Marco'*, and now have a strength of 750 troops, based at Brindisi. It is part of the navy's Underwater Raider Command (*Comando Subacque Incursori*), which controls other naval SOFs. The 'San Marcos' are organised into Operational, Logistics, and Training Gps, the first consisting of one each parachute-qualified HQ, assault, and support companies. Officers and NCOs are drawn from both the army and navy, but ORs are specially selected navy conscripts.

Like France, Italy has established a Rapid Intervention Force (*Fòrza d'Intervènto Ràpido*—FIR) composed of Pcht.Bde. '*Folgore*', Motorised Bde. '*Friuli*', Naval Bn. '*San Marco*', and an AF transport squadron; other support units may be attached.

Greece
Greece's first SOF unit was the British-backed, parachute-

An Italian 'Folgore' Parachute Brigade *sergente-maggiore* (left) carries out a pre-jump inspection of a Portuguese paratrooper during a joint NATO exercise. (MSgt. W.B.Belcher, USAF)

trained Sacred Sdn., formed in 1942 and composed entirely of former regular officers. It conducted raids with the SAS in North Africa and later with the SBS in the Aegean. A US-advised jump school was established in 1955 outside Athens. Parachute and commando units began to form; and eventually an entire Para-Cdo.Div. was established, consisting of: Para Regt.—2 Para Bns. & 1 SRF Bn.; Cdo.Regt.—3 Cdo.Bns.; and Marine Inf.Regt.—3 Marine Battalions.

Each regiment also has a light artillery battalion; and there are various divisional support units. The regiments, besides executing their special missions, can also be employed as light infantry, with the exception of the Special Raider Force Bn. which continues the lineage of the Sacred Sdn. and has both direct action and LRRP rôles. Its six man teams operate in a unique manner, each being composed of three career NCOs paired with a conscript. Since Greece enjoys one of NATO's longest conscription periods—24 months—these ORs can become fairly well versed in their trade while under the tutelage of experienced NCOs. The Para-Cdo. Div's. 32nd Marine Inf.Regt., an army unit, is principally trained to conduct small island operations in the Aegean Sea. The author once asked an SRF NCO if there were any mountain units in the Greek Army, he replied, 'In my country we are all mountain troops'.

Spain
During the Civil War both the Germans and Soviets trained

small Spanish **parachute** units, neither of which made a combat jump. The air force formed a small unit in 1946 and still has three company-sized units, including the Pcht. Sapper Sdn. intended for seizing airfields. The army did not form its I Bn. and school until 1953, which made its first jump on 23 February 1954, now considered the *Paracaidistas* formation day. II Bn. was formed in 1956, and by 1957 both units were to see action in Morocco. III Bn. was formed in 1960, and the Pcht. Depot and Instruction Unit was established at Murcia in 1961. *Brigada Paracaidista* (BRIPAC) was organised in February 1965 in Madrid. Support units were activated over the years; and the BRIPAC, with about 4,500 troops, is now composed of:

HQ, Pcht.Bde. (*Cuartel General de la BRIPAC*)—1965
I Bn.Pcht. 'Roger de Flor'—1953[1]
II Bn.Pcht. 'Roger de Lauria'—1956
III Bn.Pcht. 'Ortiz de Zarate'—1960
Arty.Gp. (*Grupo de Artilleria*)—1966
Mixed Engineer Bn. (*Batallón Mixto de Ingenieros*)—1957
Logistics Gp. (*Grupo Logistico*)—1965
Drop & Air Transport Gp. (*Grupo de Lanzamiento y Aerotransporte*)—1987
Pcht. Services Unit (*Unidad de Servicios Paracaidista*)—1964
Pcht. Instruction Bn. (*Batallón de Instrucción Paracaidista*)—1971
Hunter (AT) Co. (*Companía Cazacarros*)—1987

SOFs include six **special operations groups** (*Grupo de la*

[1]The parachute battalions are designated *Bandera* (rather than *Batallón de Paracaidistas* and consist of HQ, support, and 4 infantry companies. Groups are battalion-sized.

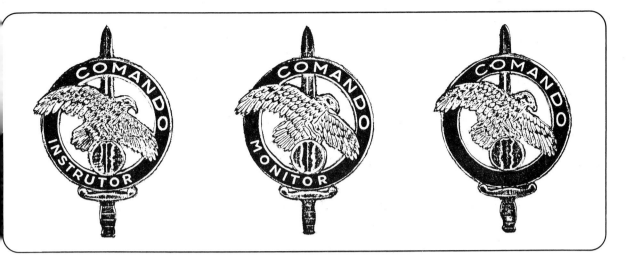

Operationes Especiales—GOE), one per military region, intended for local defence, with two special operations companies (*Companía de las Operationes Especiales*—COE) known as '*Guerilleros*'. Other GOEs are assigned to the Ceuta and Melilla General Commands on the Moroccan coast as well as the Balearic Islands. Two special sea companies (*Companía de las Mar Especiales*) are based on the Canary Islands with a similar mission, but are also small-boat trained.

Jump-master of the Spanish Parachute Brigade checks the rig of a member of the Mixed Engineer Battalion. The red/yellow/red national flash is worn on the left shoulder above the battalion patch; the brigade patch on the right shoulder. (Official)

Spain also has an airmobile 4,000-man Air Transport Bde. (*Brigada Aerotransporte*—BRIAT) organised similarly to the BRIPAC. The BRIPAC, BRIAT, and other units constitute the General Reserve Force. Spain has recently announced that it will form a multi-service Rapid Action Force (*Fuerza Acción Rápido*—FAR) composed of the BRIPAC, BRIAT, TEAR, 21st Fighter and 31st Transport Wings, and other units.

Intended to protect Spanish interests, it is orientated towards the Canary and Balearic Islands, Straits of Gibraltar, and the Spanish sovereign towns of Ceuta and Melilla, disputed by Morocco. Other SPFs include 4th 'Urgel' and 6th 'Navarra'

Mountain Divs. and the High Mountain Bde. in the Pyrenees. The divisions each have two brigades with substantial brigade and divisional support units.

Spain was the first nation to form **marines**. The navy's *Infanteria de Marina* (IdM) have gone through a bewildering number of reorganisations and name changes since their inception in 1537. They have fought on almost every continent and executed some 30 landings, their first in 1541, with another of interest at Pensacola, Florida in 1770. The current organisation, adopted in 1968, is composed of units known as

Shoulder patches of the Spanish Parachute Brigade – BRIPAC; all are black on olive in their subdued field presentation. *Top, l. to r.*: Parachute Bde.; Bde. HQ; Parachute Instruction Bn. *Centre, l. to r.*: I Bn. 'Roger de Flor'; II Bn. 'Roger de Lauria'; III Bn. 'Ortiz de Zarate'. *Bottom, l. to r.*: Artillery Group; Mixed Engineer Bn.; Logistics Group. (C&D)

Spanish marines of the Special Operations Unit conduct a rubber boat infiltration exercise. Their berets are black, with a gold anchor badge; they appear to wear standard olive fatigues. (Official)

Tercio (literally 'one third', the traditional term for a regiment) or *Agrupción* (group), each organised in the same way and carrying on the lineages of past units. These 'light regiments' consist of an HQ, base and security battalions, naval police and band, providing navy base security. The 11,900-man IdM are deployed as follows:

Comandancia General—Madrid
Tercio del Norte (North)—El Ferrol
Tercio del Sur (South)—San Fernando
Tercio de Levante (East)—Cartagena
Agrupación de Madrid—Madrid
Agrupación de Canarias (Canary Is.)—Las Palmas
Centro de Instrucción (Instruction Centre)—Cartagena
Escuela de Aplicación (Applications School)—San Fernando

The IdM's operational force is the *Tercio de Armada* (TEAR), a 3,000-man brigade based at San Fernando. Formed in 1969, it is a modern amphibious assault force consisting of: HQ, TEAR (*Cuatel General de la TEAR*); Landing Gp. (*Agrupación de Desembarco*); Combat Support Gp. (*Agrupación Apoyo Combate*); Special Operations Unit (*Unidad Operaciones Especiales*); Combat Logistics Gp. (*Grupo Logistico Combate*); and Base Unit (*Unidad Base*).

The component groups are all battalion-sized. The UOE is a parachute and combat swimmer trained commando unit thought to be of large company size.

The 7,000-man brigade-sized Spanish Legion[1] (which no longer accepts foreigners and is being further reduced in size), of four *Tercios* may be included in the FAR. In 1985 the Special Operations Co., formed in 1981, was enlarged to a battalion. It is subordinate to 4th *Tercio* 'Alejandro de Farnesio', along with a light cavalry group, and based at the Legion's main depot at Ronda. It is expected that the 3rd *Tercio* 'Juan de Austria' will be moved from the Canary Islands to Ronda and its two motorised infantry battalions converted to airmobile. The 1st 'Gran Capitán' and 2nd Duque de Alba *Tercios*, each with motorised and mechanised infantry battalions and a new AT company, are based at Melilla and Ceuta, Morocco, respectively.

Portugal

The original **parachute** cadre were trained in France and Spain in 1951 and 1953 respectively. The troops of the planned para battalion undertook jump training in Spain in 1955, and the Pcht. Light Inf., or 'Hunter', Bn. (*Batalhão Cacadores Pára-quedistas*—BCP) was activated on 14 August 1955 (Infantry Day). By 1956 it was fully organised and stationed at Air Force Base 3 at Tancos. A jump school was established in 1957. With the growth of rebellion in Portugal's African colonies, the BCP's three companies were dispatched to Angola in 1961. Once there the three companies were formed into a new unit, BCP 21 based at Luanda. The original BCP was expanded to the *Regimento Cacadores Pára-quedistas* in December 1961 and tasked with training additional BCPs for Africa:

BCP 12—Guinea-Bissau (1966–74)
BCP 21—Angola (1961–75)
BCP 22—Portugal (1962–76)
BCP 30—Portugal (1962–76)
BCP 31—Mozambique (1962–75)
BCP 32—Mozambique (1966–74)

Small-scale combat jumps were made in the colonies and large numbers of specialised units were formed to counter the guerrillas, but to no avail.[2] In 1975 the Para Regt. was disbanded and replaced by the Paratroops School Base (*Base Escola de Tropas de Pára*—BETP). In 1976 the *Brigada Cacadores Pára-quedistas* was formed consisting of the BETP, *Base Operaciones de Tropas de Pára No 1* (BOTP-1) at Monsanto-Lisbon, and BOTP-2 at San Jacinto-Aveiro.

A Special Operations School had been opened in Lamego to

[1]See MAA 161, *The Spanish Foreign Legion.*

[2]See MAA 202, *Modern African Wars (2): Angola and Moçambique 1961–74.*

conduct a ten week commando course for officers and NCOs destined for Africa. Later schools were opened in the colonies to better prepare them for service in one of the 67 commando companies (*Companhias de Comandos*). Portugal withdrew and granted independence to Guinea in 1974 and Mozambique, Cape Verde and Angola in 1975. On 1 May 1975 the *Regimento de Comandos* was formed at Lamego with 11 and 12 Cdo.Bns. (five cos. each), Service and Instruction Bns., and a signal company. It is now part of the 2,000-man Special Forces Bde. (*Brigada de Forca Especial*) formed on 3 July 1984.

The SF Bde. will be augmented in wartime by conventional combat and support units as well as the 1,800-man Para Bde., with two battalions and two separate companies. The paras are now made up of army and air force personnel under air force control.

The Portuguese **marines** date back to 1585, and, like their Spanish counterparts, have fought in all of Portugal's wars; some 13,000 served in the African colonies. Known as the Navy Fusiliers (*Fuzileiros Navais*), today's marines number 2,500 navy personnel forming a naval police and two amphibious assault battalions with HQ in Lisbon.

Yugoslavia

Little information is available on the Yugoslav 36th Pcht. Bde., in fact inquiries to the Yugoslav Embassy were met by the suggestion that the author request information from the US Embassy in Belgrade. The Brigade was formed in the 1950s and based in Nis. Yugoslavia also possesses a 2,000-man Naval Inf. Bde. (*Mornaricka Pesadijska Brigada*) in the vicinity of the Bay of Cattaro, as well as one mountain brigade trained in guerrilla warfare methods; all types of brigades have three battalions.

Middle East

Both US and British influence is seen in this region's SOFs; but as turmoil continues without the direct involvement of outside nations, these states have begun to follow their own path.

Iran

Under the Shah's regime the nation's SOFs and SPFs received extensive training and support from the US. These units included the 25th Pcht. and SF Bdes., some of the latter being sent in 1972–74 to aid Oman. There were also ranger and mountain units. Iranian forces at the time were considered among the best trained in the Middle East. Within months of the Shah's 1979 downfall they were mere shadows of their former selves, demonstrating what a perishable asset combat readiness actually is. Little information has come to light on current Iranian SOFs, but it is reported that an SF division of four brigades is in operation, used principally as shock troops. Of the original SOFs, much of their experienced manpower was squandered early in the Gulf War in senseless frontal attacks. Now, at least some of the SF units are employed fighting Kurdish rebels. The *basij*—volunteers of the Islamic Revolutionary Guards Corps (*Pasdaran Inqilab*) are by no means considered an SOF organisation, although they are reported to contain some parachute and commando units.

A rare photograph of Yugoslavia's 36th Parachute Brigade; these men wear jump-suits and a special issue jump helmet, while the commissioned jump-master wears the OD beret illustrated in Plate E4. (Official)

They primarily serve the Ayatollah Khomeini by willingly accepting martyrdom in fanatical attacks.

Iraq

Iraq had a small airborne unit in the late 1940s, but it was not until 1964 that the foundations for the present SOF structure were laid. USSF teams began airborne training, and an SF brigade soon evolved, elements of which fought the Israelis in 1973. The SOFs were greatly expanded early in the Gulf War, and it is now reported that there is one commando and six SF brigades. However, in 1987 it was reported that one commando brigade was in action on the Northern Front, two (1st and 66th) on the North Central Front, and an SF brigade on the Central Front: due to translation difficulties it is easy to confuse Arabic unit designations. Iraq is also reported to have conducted several combat jumps during the war, the most recent being a brigade-sized operation to cut off Iranian forces holding the Majnun Islands in June 1988.

Jordan

Jordan's small army has always maintained a reputation as one of the best-trained Arab forces, and the same applies to its SOFs. A British-trained parachute company was formed in 1963; but full effectiveness was not seen until USSF training was introduced in 1967, to be followed by the activation of the Special Services Gp. on 30 June 1969. Initially not all elements were airborne, but in the mid-1970s the unit was redesignated the SF 'Saiqa' (Storm) Bde. and personnel of its three 500-man battalions undertake six months of intensive training including a nine-week ranger course followed by a three-week jump school. (These are also available to non-SF personnel and required of all military academy cadets.) Membership in the SF Bde. is limited to 'East Bank' bedouins to ensure loyalty to the king. The SF Bde. is based near Zarqa, and is today exclusively US-equipped. One battalion (101st) was trained by the British SAS in a CT rôle; another served in Oman in the late 1970s. The US has suggested the SF Bde. be expanded to two and employed as a mobile Arab regional 'peacekeeping' force—an idea which simply enthralled Israel. . .

Oman

The Sultan of Oman maintains excellent British-advised armed forces. In 1974 volunteers from the Oman Gendarmerie were jump trained in Saudi Arabia, forming the company-sized D (Pcht.) Sdn. in 1975. The Omanis opened their own Parachute Training School in 1977; and in 1978 the unit, now part of the army, was redesignated the Oman Pcht. Sdn. at Rustaq; it was enlarged to a regiment (bn.) in the mid-1980s. Besides the army, navy and air force, Oman has another armed force, the Sultan's Royal Household, composed of the Royal Guard Bde., Royal Yacht, Royal Flight, and the Sultan's Special Force. The Sultan's SF is a 400-man battalion-sized unit advised by the British SAS. Its personnel are recruited exclusively from the inhabitants of the *jebel* area of Dhofar and are trained in typical SAS skills including LRRP, small boat and long-range desert motorised operations.

Saudi Arabia

Though Saudi Arabia formed a small British-trained airborne unit in the late 1950s, operating with the British in Kuwait in 1961, it was not until the mid-1960s that expansion was to take place with assistance from the USSF. Each of the armed forces, plus para-military organisations such as the National Guard and police, now have some form of airborne unit: the relevant

A marine of Italy's 'San Marco' Battalion in shirtsleeve order during deployment to Lebanon as part of the MNF in 1983. The unit's 'St. Mark's Lion' badge is here worn on the chest – cf. Plate D5.

ministries are each under the control of a member of the royal family, with each desiring to have their own special unit. The army's, the only one of serious military significance, is the Abn.Bde. composed of two parachute battalions and three Special Troops companies (SF-type units). Some of the latter fought the Israelis in 1973 on the Golan Heights.

Syria
A parachute company was formed in 1958; expanded to a battalion, it was sent to Egypt as an element of a joint Egyptian–Syrian brigade. With the dissolving of the United Arab Republic, the unit returned home in 1960. The commando battalions were an outgrowth of this unit. Though Syria is heavily supported by the Soviet Union, its SOFs are more akin to Egypt's than to Russian models, i.e. they are employed in large numbers and often as shock troops. They are also employed as anti-tank troops, well equipped with wire-guided missiles and rocket launchers, and infiltrated into Israeli rear areas by foot and helicopter to execute anti-armour ambushes. They have also been heavily involved in the Lebanon since 1976; and in the early 1980s the Pcht.Bn. was increased to brigade strength.

The Cdo., or SF (*al-Wahdat al-Khassa*) Bde. was increased to as many as 30 battalions, ten of which were deployed in the Beka'a Valley in 1982. The small commando battalions are organised into groups (*fu'gj*) usually of three each. Not all are parachute trained, and many are employed to secure vital installations and facilities within Syria. They are required to be members of the Alawite sect to ensure loyalty. The number of commando battalions is now thought to have been reduced, and the Pcht. and Cdo.Bdes. consolidated into an SF Div. Another SOF organisation are the Defence Companies (*Saraya ad-Difa*—'Defenders of the Regime'), which have a commando rôle and are generally parachute trained; they too are all Alawite.

Turkey
The various Turkish SPFs were initially trained by the US and employ US organisation and early-model equipment. There can be little doubt, considering the Turkish soldier's fearsome reputation, that their training is tough. In the early 1970s there were only three parachute battalions; today there are the Pcht.Bde. (*Parasütcü Piyade*) and two para-commando brigades (*Parasütcü Komando Piyade*). Each 5,000-man brigade has three para or para-commando battalions plus one of artillery and supporting units. They have been employed on bandit-hunting expeditions and opium-burning campaigns within their country's rugged interior, as well as border security missions. A complete brigade conducted a parachute and helicopter assault on Cyprus during the invasion of 1974.

The Amphibious Rifle Bde. (*Amfibi Deniz Piyade*) is a 4,000-man navy unit with the same basic organisation as the above brigades. It too was originally trained by the US Marines, and has principally US equipment. Elements of this unit also took part in the Cyprus operation.

North Yemen
The Yemen Arab Republic (pro-West) is extremely sensitive about its SOFs. The first North Yemeni paratroopers were trained by Egyptian instructors in 1964; the small unit grew to

Turkish para-commando in fighting order, with G3 rifle. This is the 'duck-hunter' camouflage uniform illustrated in Plate F5. The webbing equipment is olive green. (P.N.R.Thomas)

company size by the late 1960s, then into a battalion, and finally into a brigade by the late 1970s. The brigade commander defected, along with several hundred of his troops, to the People's Republic of Yemen (South) in 1978. The following year these same troops participated in the South Yemeni invasion of the North, though they were soon withdrawn after a cease-fire agreement. The para brigade, '*Al Mithallat*' Bde., is now actually only a large battalion based at Madhalat Camp in Sana'a, with an element in Taiz. The 8th '*Saiqa*' (Storm) Bde. is composed of an SF and two commando battalions, but not all elements are parachute trained. (No information is available on South Yemeni SOFs; it is not even known if any exist.)

North Africa

Although the French, British, and Italians have had a certain amount of influence in this region, little of it can be seen today in the local SOFs.

Djibouti

The French, who maintain a garrison (13th Foreign Legion Demi-Bde.) in what was formerly French Somaliland, first trained parachutists in 1979; a 30-man para company was formed in November 1980. The next year instructors were trained in France and the unit expanded; it is based at Camp Lattelier near the capital. The base's main tenant is the Cdo. Intervention Regt. (bn.), but the para company is under direct control of the army's commanding general. The high-quality 160-man unit runs its own jump school.

Egypt

Egypt was the first Arab country to form an airborne unit, even establishing facilities to manufacture parachutes; using British aid, the jump school was opened by the air force in June 1951. The first class graduated a year later and the school transferred to the army. Three companies were formed, and consolidated in the 1st Pcht.Bn. on 9 September 1954. A two-battalion Pcht.Bde. was formed on 21 August 1958, which included a Syrian battalion based in Egypt during the two year existence of the United Arab Republic. With the departure of the Syrian unit the 2nd Pcht.Bn. was formed in June 1961, followed by the 3rd in September, along with an artillery unit. The 4th and 5th Pcht.Bns. were formed in 1964, the 4th to serve in Yemen; there was also a short-lived reserve battalion in 1967. The further establishment of airborne units becomes muddled at this point due to the security restrictions imposed during the conflicts with Israel. A second parachute brigade was formed in the early 1970s, along with an airmobile brigade under the control of the Air Landing HQ. These units all fought in the 1973 war and are still in existence: 140th and 182nd Pcht. and 170th Ambl. Brigades.

Commando units were also formed in the 1960s, growing to 28 battalions by 1973; some serving in Yemen. These were organised under the Special Forces HQ (*As-Sa'iqa* or 'Lightning') into the 1,000-man 127th–133rd Cdo.Gps. of four small battalions each. Their principal rôle in the 1973 war was to infiltrate, usually by helicopter, across the Canal and interdict units moving to the front by anti-armour ambush deep in the Sinai. Another SPF unit was the army's 130th Amph.Bde., the first Arab unit to conduct an amphibious

A member of Egypt's 182nd Parachute Brigade instructs a US 82nd Airborne Division soldier on the RPG-7V rocket-launcher during a 'Bright Star' exercise. He wears the green padded jump helmet and reversible camouflage uniform – cf. Plate G3. (US Army)

operation, crossing Little Bitter Lake in 1973 to support the commandos.[1]

Ethiopia

With the establishment of the Provisional Military Government of Socialist Ethiopia in 1977, there was a general reorganisation and expansion of the armed forces under the guidance of Soviet, Cuban, and East German advisors. The existing parachute brigade and four divisional commando companies, originally trained by Israel and USSF, were expanded to four para-commando brigades. The old jump school and brigade were at Debre Zeit, but locations of the current units are classified. They have been employed against the Somalis and rebel groups in the north.

Libya

A parachute company was trained by Egypt in 1971 and soon went to Syria for further parachute and commando training. A jump school was established at Ukba bin Naf'i, and by 1976 the unit was of battalion size. It was to see action against Egypt the following year, in Chad in 1978, and in Uganda in 1979. It was expanded to a small Cdo.-Para Bde. in the early 1980s with its units based throughout Libya. With further conflicts in Chad and the perceived threat of an American invasion, the brigade

[1] See MAA 194, *Arab Armies of the Middle East Wars (2)*.

was expanded to an estimated 14 battalions, one of which is part of Gaddafi's bodyguard.

Somalia
The first parachute unit was formed in the early 1970s with Soviet aid and a jump school established at Balidogle Air Base. When the Soviets were expelled in 1978 the parachute capability eroded, with the last jump being made just prior to the Soviet expulsion. Some jumpers were trained in other countries, but today's 6th Cdo.Regt. is principally a ground unit based at Balidogle. There are reports that there are four such battalion-sized units.

Sudan
In 1962 a cadre of Sudanese were trained in England and the Pcht.Bn. was formed. Their first combat jump was to take place in 1965. The Pcht. Training Centre was established in 1964 and the battalion expanded to a brigade in the late 1960s. The jump school and 144th Pcht.Bde. are located at the Armed Forces HQ in Khartoum and are directly under the Airborne Corps HQ, the commander of which is a member of the ruling Transitional Military Council. The 144th also includes small LRRP and CT units. It has seen combat against rebels in the south.

The British influence is clear in this photo of members of the Kenyan Parachute Battalion – Denison smocks, Mk II jump helmet with painted jump-wings, and British-supplied parachutes. (Jon B.Crane)

Central & Southern Africa

Angola
When Angola became independent of Portugal in 1975 it had no established airborne forces. A unit was formed in about 1976 with the aid of Cuban Assault and Landing Troops and Soviet advisors; some assistance may later have been supplied by Portugal. The Pcht.Bn. is under the control of the People's Air Force/Air Defence and principally employed as a presidential guard, but has seen some combat against UNITA rebels.

Kenya
A para company was formed on 26 April 1965 and trained as a body in England that same year. The unit was expanded to the Para Bn. in 1982. Tasked with a commando rôle, it sometimes works with the 50th Air Cavalry Bn., equipped with light attack helicopters. British jump instructors worked with the unit until 1970 and again in the mid-1970s.

South Africa
A small cadre was trained in all aspects of **parachute** operations in England in 1960. This group formed the core of 2 Mobile Watch (bn.) that same year. On 1 April 1961 it was redesignated and reorganised as 1 Para Bn. (1 *Valskermbattaljon*). Late in the year a jump school was established at Tempe Airfield, Bloemfontein. In 1966 1 Para was to be the first South

African unit to see combat since World War II when it was committed against guerrillas. The unit then consisted of an HQ, two Permanent Force (PF) companies and four of the Citizen Force (CF-reserves). In 1971 2 Para Bn. was formed as a CF unit, and 1 Para's companies increased to four of PF; both units were based at Bloemfontein. Personnel completing their active duty were assigned to 2 Para, which also saw combat in 1975–76.

The South African Army was reorganised in the early 1970s and this placed 2 Para under 1 Corps HQ, which controlled all Conventional Forces. The CF's 3 Para Bn. was formed in 1977 in Johannesburg and 2 Para relocated to Pretoria. Companies from all three battalions were to rotate through South West Africa (now Namibia) serving as CI reaction forces; a few small-scale combat jumps were made.

In 1978 1 Corps was disbanded (since reformed) and all Conventional Force units placed directly under the Chief of the Army. It was decided that the para battalions should be formed into a combined arms force to make them more effective. On 20 April 1978 44 Para Bde. was formed at Bloemfontein. The next month, well before it was fully formed, a company each from 2 and 3 Paras plus supporting platoons from 1 Para were hastily formed into a composite battalion and dropped on a principal SWAPO base inside Angola. The 1 Para is still a PF unit (with HQ co. & six inf.cos.) and is not part (nor is 101 Air Supply

Co.) of the all-CF 44 Bde. Now acting as the Quick Reaction Force, this consists of:

HQ, 44 Para Bde.	44 Signals, Field Workshop,
2, 3 & 4 Para Bns.	& Logistics (each
18 Light Regt. (arty.bn.)	co.-sized)
44 Anti-Aircraft Regt. (bn.)	Pathfinder Co.
44 Field Engineer Sdn. (co.)	

In late 1968 a CF unit known as Hunter Gp. was formed with a LRRP rôle and was soon redesignated as Recce Unit (Reserve). From this organisation sprang the **Recce Commando** (*Vervennings*) concept, and a number of similar PF units began to be formed in the early 1970s. Many were to see service in Rhodesia through 1975 and all operated in Angola in a CI rôle. The battalion-sized 1, 2, 4, and 5 Recce Cdo.Regts. are assigned to 1 SF Bde. at Bloemfontein, along with 32 Inf.Bn. The Recce Cdos. perform SAS-type deep penetration LRRP missions and are highly skilled in tracking, scouting, weapons, demolitions, and survival; their selection course is extremely

Shoulder badges of South Africa's 44 Parachute Brigade. All are in lucite-coated metal; the background is burgundy, the parachutes white edge with gold, and all other motifs gold outline, all within gold borders. (1) 2 Para Bn. (2) 3 Para Bn. (3) 44 Para Bde. HQ, with SA Army bar – see Plate H5. (4) 4 Para Bn. (5) 44 AA Regt. (6) 18 Light Regt., with 44 Bde. bar. (7) 44 Field Eng. Sdn. (8) 44 Sigs. (9) 44 Logistics. (10) 44 Field Workshop. (C&D)

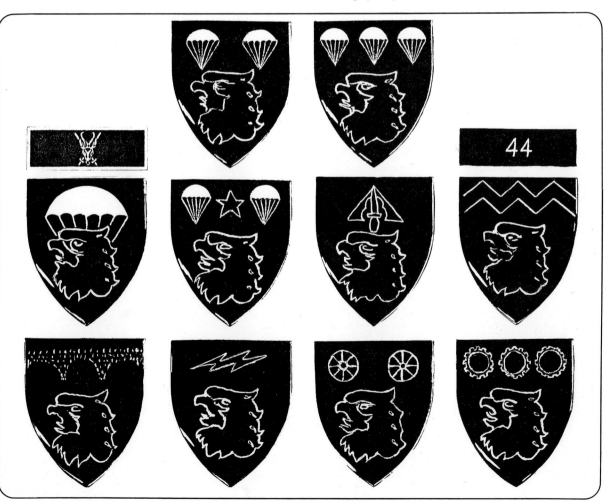

reformed as C Sdn. Rhodesian SAS at Salisbury in 1962 and based at Cranborne. The unit conducted LRRP and CI operations in Rhodesia and neighbouring Mozambique, to include joint operations with the Portuguese. The all-white unit was expanded to battalion strength in 1978, and blacks were integrated into the redesignated 1 (Rhodesian) SAS Regt., which moved to Kabrit Barracks in 1979.

The Selous Scouts were a racially integrated battalion-sized LRRP and CI unit formed in 1974 with an SAS cadre. Selection standards were brutal, and their combat missions no less so. The often controversial 'Scouts' specialised in cross-border operations, often posing as ZANLA and ZIPRA guerrillas. The unit conducted a large number of small parachute infiltration missions as did the SAS.

The Rhodesian Light Inf. (a commando unit with one company parachute trained) and Grey's Scouts were battalion-sized CI units with high selection standards. Both were integrated and proved to be extremely effective in their own styles of CI warfare. The RLI ran small unit hit-and-run raids and ambushes, while Grey's conducted horse-mounted bush country security and ambush patrols.

With black majority rule established in 1980 and the country

Various publications have identified this soldier as a Libyan (doubtful) or a Lebanese paratrooper (impossible). Many knowledgeable individuals have failed to identify him exactly; but he remains a fine example of a paratrooper of a Soviet-client African state. He is armed with an AK-47, and is unrigging an air-dropped B-10 82mm recoilless gun.

South African Recce Commando shoulder badges. All are black and white; they are made both in cloth and in lucite-coated metal. (1) 1 Regt. (2) 2 Regt. (3) Recce Unit (Reserve). (4) 4 Regt. (5) 5 Regt. (6) Beret badge – burgundy ground, gold wreath, black and silver compass rose (Intelligence symbol). (C&D)

demanding and conducted in an operational environment. The 32 Inf.Bn. is another special CI unit, composed mainly of Angolan personnel for behind-the-lines reconnaissance and DA missions.

Some of the nine 'independent states and self-governing homelands', made up of different tribal groups and located within the geographical confines of South Africa, have formed small airborne units with South African aid and support. These units, from platoon to battalion size, are trained in CI and CT operations. The largest of these is the Namibia Para Bn. at Leiperdsvallei.

Zimbabwe

Rhodesia's contribution to the Malayan emergency took the form of a group of volunteers which made up C Sdn., Malayan Scouts (SAS) formed in Johore, Malaya in 1951. Redesignated C Sdn., 22 SAS in 1952, the unit served there until the following year when it returned to Rhodesia and disbanded. When insurgent groups began to wage guerrilla warfare the unit was now called Zimbabwe, these excellent units were dissolved on paper to pacify their former enemies; but the cadres, blacks and some whites, were to form new units with basically the same rôles and methods of operations. Interestingly both ZANLA and ZIPRA troops (themselves not exactly brothers-in-arms) are integrated into these new units, serving shoulder-to-shoulder with some of their former enemies:

Rhodesia	Zimbabwe
Selous Scouts & some SAS	1 Pcht.Bn. (1,000 men)
Rhodesian Light Inf.	1 Cdo.Bn. (1,000 men)
Grey's Scouts	1 Mounted Inf.Bn. (800 men)

A more recent addition to the Zimbabwe National Army is 5th Inf.Bde. 'Gukurahundi' (People's Storm). Formed in mid-1981 solely from ZANLA troops, this 5,000-man special CI formation was trained by North Koreans, though two of its battalions had been trained by the British. It was to operate outside the normal army command structure, and was kept isolated at Inyanga Base on the mountainous Mozambique border. It is the army's only mechanised force and is composed of three infantry, one tank and one artillery battalions plus support units. Operational in June 1982, this controversial formation was used only for 'disturbances' and was soon terrorizing the country side to keep dissidents in line and

Troopers of 6 Bn., Royal Australian Regiment swap their khaki infantry berets for maroon in December 1983 when the unit officially received parachute status. The officers appear to be armed with AR-15 rifles, the ORs with FAL L1A1s; both are currently being replaced with the Austrian Steyr AUG.A1 (Official)

seeking retribution from old tribal enemies. It was soon apparent that the North Koreans were doing a poor job, and they were sent home in 1983; British advisors took over the unit's training, but it is still often charged with brutality.

Far East and Asia

Extensive British influence can be seen throughout this region, though USSF assistance to many of the regional SOFs can be detected.

Australia

The 1 Para Bn. plus other small units were formed in 1943, but these were disbanded at the war's end without seeing action. The air force established a jump school in 1951, but while personnel from all services undertook the training, they simply returned to their units.

The 1 SAS Co., Australian SAS was formed in July 1957 in Swanbourne, Western Australia using individuals who had served with the British SAS in Malaya. In 1960 1 SAS Co. was made a component of the Royal Australian Regt. (RAR), until 1st ASAS Regt. was formed in 1964 with 1 and 2 Squadrons[1].

[1]SAS units organised along British lines are composed of 'sabre squadrons', each with a small HQ and several 'troops', each troop specialising in a specific skill, i.e. freefall, mountain, small boat, scuba, desert mobile, etc. A troop normally has four 'patrols' each of four or five men.

In 1965 1 Sdn. was deployed to Brunei (British possession on N. Borneo) and began operations against Indonesian forces, to be withdrawn in 1966. The year 1965 also saw the first ASAS elements sent to Vietnam, where they operated with the USSF; 3 Sdn. was formed and sent to Vietnam in April 1966. All three squadrons subsequently served two, approximately one-year tours until October 1971; they principally provided LRRP support to the 1st Australian Task Force. Today's 1st ASAS Regt. is composed of HQ; 1, 2 and 3 SAS; Base; and 151 (Signals) Sdns. at Campbell Barracks, Swanbourne. Their training is similar to that of the British SAS with whom they maintain a relationship, but structured to Australia's unique needs and character.

The 1 Cdo. City of Sydney's Own Regt. was formed as a Citizen Military Force (reserves) unit at about the same time as 1 SAS Co., maintaining close ties with the ASAS, many of whose personnel transferred to it upon leaving active duty. On 1 February 1980 it was redesignated 1st Cdo.Regt. and made a

Paratroopers of the Chinese People's Liberation Army parading in 1984. They wear new green uniforms with red collar tabs, unidentified silver badges on the shoulder straps, white scarfs, and large right sleeve patches – see Plate I2a. (DIA)

component of the Special Action Forces, which includes the ASAS. The regiment is tasked with direct action missions and specialises in small boat and mountain operations. Its two commandos are actually large companies. It is manned by ASAS regular cadres and reserve personnel. Reservists must complete basic and infantry training, commando selection, jump and small craft handling courses plus their trade tests, usually taking up to two years. They then specialise as either divers or climbers; the former taking the shallow water diver and beach recce courses, and the latter the rock climbing and cliff leader courses, with both taking the roping and rapelling course. Later, all take the submarine familiarisation, industrial sabotage and demolition, and advanced unarmed combat courses. Even more advanced instructor courses are available to NCOs. HQ, 1st Cdo.Regt. is at Canberra; 1 Cdo. at Sydney; 2 Cdo. at Williamstown; and 126 Signals Sdn. at Watsonia.

The original air force school at Williamstown was taken over by the army in 1974 and moved to Her Majesty's Air Station Albatross (a navy base at Nowra), re-opening in February 1986 as the Pcht. Training Centre. Also in 1974, Co.D, 6th Bn. RAR was placed on jump status until 3rd Bn. (Para) RAR, at Holsworthy barracks outside Sydney, assumed that rôle in December 1983.

See plates commentaries for details.

1: Belgium: 2 Bn., Para-Commando Regt.
2: Belgium: 1 ESR Co., Para-Commando Regt.

3: France: 13^e RDP
4: France: 2^e RPIMa
5: France: 27^e BCA
6: France: GFMC

A

See plates commentaries for details.

1: Netherlands: 104 R&S Co.
2: Netherlands: KN Korps Mariniers
3: W. Germany: 300 Fernspähkompanie
4: W. Germany: 23 Gebirgsjägerbrigade
5: Switzerland: Fernspähkompanie 17
6: Canada: Canadian Abn. Regt.

B

4a

4

JÄGARE 4b

JÄGARE 4c

3a

3

JÆGER

PATRULJE

1

1a

See plates commentaries for details.

1: Finland: Coastal Ranger Bn.
2: Finland: Abn. Jaeger School
3: Denmark: Jaegerkorpset
4: Sweden: Lapland Jaeger Regt.

2

2a

6

KA 1

KUSTJÄGARNA

6b

5a

5b

5

6a

5: Sweden: Para-Jaeger School
6: Sweden: Coastal Jaeger School

C

See plates commentaries for details.

1: Norway: Jaeger School
2: Norway: Naval Jaeger Co.

3: Italy: 9 Para-Raider Bn.
4: Italy: Alpine Bde. 'Tridentina'

5: Italy: Marine Bn. 'San Marco'
6: Greece: Special Raider Force Bn.

D

See plates commentaries for details.

1: Spain: 2 Parachute Bn.
2: Spain: 101 Spec. Ops. Co.
3: Portugal: Commando Regt.
4: Yugoslavia: 36 Para Bde.
5: Iraq: 66th Commando Bde.
6: Iran: SF Division

E

See plates commentaries for details.

1: Jordan, SF Bde.
2: Oman: Sultan's SF

3: Saudi Arabia: Abn. Bde.
4: Syria: Commando Bde.

5: Turkey: Para-Cdo. Bde.
6: Turkey: Amphib. Inf. Bde.

F

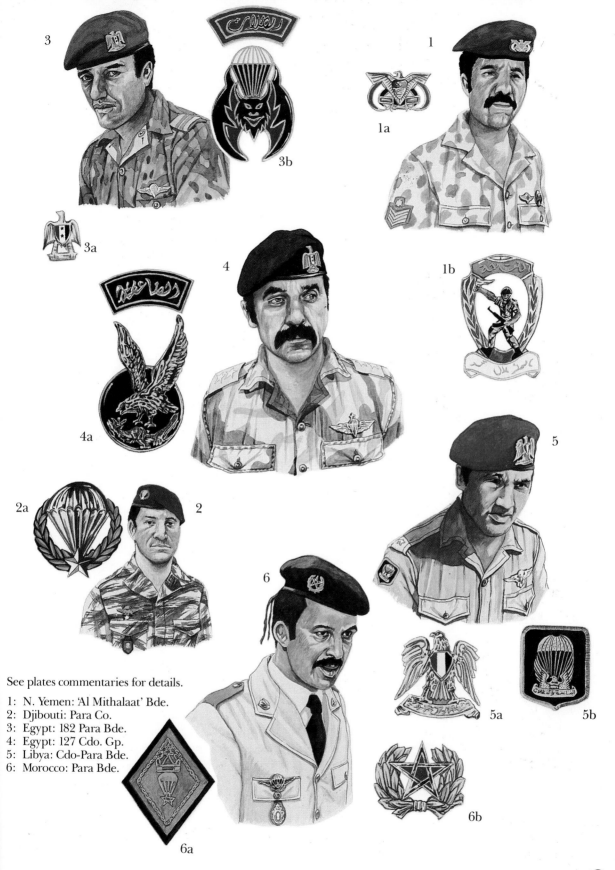

See plates commentaries for details.

1: N. Yemen: 'Al Mithalaat' Bde.
2: Djibouti: Para Co.
3: Egypt: 182 Para Bde.
4: Egypt: 127 Cdo. Gp.
5: Libya: Cdo-Para Bde.
6: Morocco: Para Bde.

G

See plates commentaries for details.

1: Somalia: 6 Cdo. Regt.
2: Sudan: 144 Para Bde.

3: Angola: Para Bn.
4: Kenya: Para Bn.

5: S. Africa: 44 Para Bde.
6: Zimbabwe: 1 Para Bn.

H

See plates commentaries for details.

1: Australia: 3 (Para) Bn. RAR
2: China: 1 Abn. Div.
3: India: Para Regt.
4: Indonesia: Para-Cdo. Regt.
5: Japan: 1 Abn. Bde.
6: S. Korea: 11 SF Bde.

I

See plates commentaries for details.

1: Malaysia: 21 Para-Cdo.
2: New Zealand: 1 NZSAS Sdn.

3: Singapore: 1 Cdo. Bn.
4: Sri Lanka: Cdo. Regt.
5: Taiwan: Commando 88
6: Thailand: 1 SF Regt.

J

See plates commentaries for details.

1: El Salvador: 1 SF Group
2: Guatemala: 1 Army Para Bn.
3: Honduras: SF Battalion
4: Nicaragua: 'Socrates Sandino' Bn.
5: Cuba: Air Assault & Landing Tps.
6: Mexico: Para-Fusilier Bde.

K

See plates commentaries for details.

1: Argentina: 601 SF Group
2: Bolivia: Para Bn.

3: Brazil: Navy SF Bn. 'Toneleros'
4: Colombia: Lancer Bn.

5: Ecuador: Naval Commando Bn.
6: Venezuela: Naval Infantry

L

China

During the post-World War II Civil War a number of Nationalist Chinese paratroopers defected to the communists. These formed the cadre for the Peoples' Republic of China's first **airborne** units, intended for the eventual invasion of Taiwan. Initially equipped by the Soviets, two divisions were in existence by the early 1960s, growing to three in the early 1970s. Though China has been involved in a number of small wars on its periphery, there have been no reports of paratroop deployment. They were used to secure critical points during periods of unrest at the time of the 'Cultural Revolution'. In recent years China has undertaken a programme to modernise its armed forces, which has led to a reduction in its massive size, but this does not seem to have affected the airborne forces. The 1st–3rd Abn.Divs. are under the 1st Abn. Corps, part of the strategic reserve, located in east central China's Jinan Military Region. They are an integral part of the air force, but once on the ground can be placed under ground forces command. Besides conventional airborne operations, for which only limited airlift is available, the airborne troops also conduct airmobile, reconnaissance, raid, and sabotage missions. Smaller SOF units are also thought to exist. The 9,100-man divisions are composed of:

Div. HQ	520	Air Defence Bty.	98
Abn. Regts. (× 3)	2,500	Guard Co.	98
Recon. Bn.	225	Signal Co.	107
Engineer Bn.	290	Chemical Co.	88
Arty.Bty.	108		

China also has a 56,500-man **naval infantry** force of nine regiments with four infantry, three tank, and three artillery battalions plus special recon. units and support elements; together forming three cadre divisions. A substantial reserve of eight divisions can be formed upon mobilisation, with 24 infantry, ten tank, and eight artillery regiments. Three active ground forces divisions are also trained for amphibious operations. While this is an impressive force, only limited-range sealift assets are available to transport just three divisions; however, there is an abundant merchant ship and motorised 'junk' fleet available to supply a sea-landed force. Successful joint amphibious operations were executed in 1955 to secure Yijiangshand (Tachen) Island, to take the Xisha (Paracel) Islands held by the South Vietnamese in 1974, and to occupy six of the Spartly Islands in January 1988, which led to sea clashes with Vietnam.

India

The 50th Indian Pcht. Bde. was formed in 1941, followed by the 44th Indian Abn.Div. in 1944, but they saw no action before VJ Day. The Indian Pcht.Regt. (IPR) was formed on 18 December 1944 as the parent unit for the division's battalions. The 44th was redesignated the 2nd in 1945; and on 26 October 1946 the IPR was disbanded, the component battalions reverting to their former designations. When Pakistan was created in 1947, the division's 14th Bde. was turned over to the new state as was the jump school at Chaklala, a new one being formed at Agra. The 50th and 77th Bdes. were retained by India, but in 1950 they were reduced to only the 50th. The IPR was re-activated on 15 April 1952, and unit designations again changed (1–4 Para Battalions).

The 50th Bde. saw action at Goa in 1961. Conflict with China in 1962 led to the formation of additional battalions between 1963–65 (5–8 Para) culminating with the formation of the 51st Pcht.Bde. in 1965. Both brigades fought in the 1965 Pakistan War, but no jumps were made. In 1966 9th Para-Cdo.Bn. was formed, followed by the 10th the next year. During the 1971 Bangladesh War both brigades and both para-commando battalions saw action. Heavily influenced by the British, the Indian paras have also displayed similar superiority in combat. In October 1987 about 50 Indian paras were airlifted into Jaffna, Sri Lanka, as part of the peacekeeping force to quell the Tamil Tiger terrorism.

Indian **mountain** divisions began to be formed in 1963 after the conflict with China demonstrated that specially conditioned, trained, equipped, and organised formations were necessary to cope with brutal Himalayan conditions. There are now nine mountain divisions and a separate brigade.

Indonesia

Paratroopers trained by the Dutch during the colonial war were to provide the cadre for three **parachute** and six parachute raider battalions in 1951–52. The Para-Cdo.Regt. (RPKAD) was formed in 1952, eventually consisting of four bn.-size groups. They and the other services' parachute units were employed over the years against rebels, mutinous armed forces, and the British in the 1963–64 Borneo confrontation. The 3,000-man Special Forces Command (KOPASSUS), evolved from the RPKAD, has a CT and two para-commando groups. There has been much restructuring over the years; there are currently the 17th and 18th Abn.Inf.Bdes. and four independent battalions, all forming a part of the Strategic Reserve Command (KOSTRAD). Each service has its own jump school. Though Indonesia has impressive airborne forces, including large police and air force units, airlift resources are limited and only small forces can be dropped.

The **marines** (KKO), on the other hand, are supported by a large number of landing craft of the navy's Military Sealift Command. The 12,000-man KKO, based at Jakarta and Surabaya, Java, consist of two infantry regiments with six bns. each, combat support, service support, and training regiments, plus an amphibious para-commando recon. unit (KIPAM).

Japan

Japan had only limited success with its army and navy parachute units in World War II. The 1st 'Kuteï' Abn.Bde. was activated in 1955 as the Ground Self Defence Force's only parachute unit; training of the unit's cadre was accomplished by the US 187th Abn.Regt'l. Combat Team. Based at Narashino under the Eastern Army, it consists of a single 1,200-man regiment with HQ, AT, and four infantry companies plus small support units. The Japanese also conduct a ranger course for other ground forces personnel, but they must first be airborne qualified.

South Korea

The Republic of Korea's (ROK) first **paratroopers** were part of United Nations Partisan Forces Korea, a highly classified SOF tasked with behind-the-lines raids and reconnaissance. Its 1st Abn.Inf.Regt. contained most of the jumpers, but there were also small parachute recon. units. More recently there were the 1st and 5th Abn.Bdes., but they and the ranger units were consolidated into the **Special Forces** in the mid-1970s. Modelled after the USSF, which still maintains an advisory presence, the SF brigades have a somewhat different organisation: HQ company and five battalions, each with four forward bases controlling four 'companies'—almost identical to a US 12-man A-team. Their training is extremely demanding and harsh by Western standards. Tae-Kwan-Do is practised almost daily, and there is frequent training in the rugged

mountain terrain and harsh weather conditions. The Special Warfare Center in Seongnam functions as a command and training centre, to include a jump school, with operational control of all SF brigades. Three are designated 'strategic' and are probably intended for cross-border direct action and reconnaissance operations; the 1st SF Bde. is known to maintain a HALO capability, the 3rd may have a land infiltration rôle, while the 5th is scuba orientated. The others are designated 'tactical' and would probably be utilised for similar missions in support of field armies and corps, in addition to organising stay-behind guerrilla forces. The ROK Army also conducts a ranger course.

1st SF Bde.—Kimpo	9th SF Bde.—Pusan
3rd SF Bde.—Seongnam	11th SF Bde.—Chunchon
5th SF Bde.—Inchon	13th SF Bde.—Uichonbu
7th SF Bde.—Iri	

The ROK **Marine** Corps was formed at Toy Hoa in 1949 under the guidance of the US Marines; by the eve of the Korean War it had grown to two battalions. During the war it grew further to the 1st Marine Corps Regt. and some independent battalions. The 2nd Marine Corps Regt. was formed in 1954, after the war, followed the next year by the 1st Marine Corps Div.; the regiments were later redesignated brigades. In October 1965 the 2nd Marine Corps Bde., the 'Blue Dragons', arrived in Vietnam with four battalions, performing excellently until departing in February 1972. Today there are 25,000 marines formed into 1st and 2nd Divs., a separate brigade, and support units.

Malaysia

British instructors assisted in 1967 with the formation of the Malaysian jump school, which gradually grew into the Malaysian Special Services Regt. (MSSR), located near Tentera with the Special Services Joint Warfare Training Centre. The MSSR is composed of 21 and 22 Para-Cdos. (bns.); there may now be a 23. There is also the Ranger Regt. (*Rejimen Renjer*), a non-airborne, light infantry unit. All of these units are highly skilled in jungle warfare and survival. The Malaysian air force possesses sufficient airlift to support them.

New Zealand

The army had no parachute units until June 1955 when the company-sized Independent New Zealand SAS Sdn. was raised. In December it was sent to Malaya and placed under the British 22 SAS as simply 'NZ Sdn.'; jump training was conducted in Singapore and jungle training in Malaya. Though effective, the unit was disbanded when it returned home in December 1957. In December 1959 an SAS troop was activated, and enlarged to a squadron the next year; training assistance was provided by the Australian SAS. A territorial (reserve) troop was formed in 1961. In May 1962 an NZSAS detachment went to Thailand and worked with USSF and Thai rangers, returning in September. To commemorate two Maori Wars units, the Forest Rangers and Taranaki Rangers,

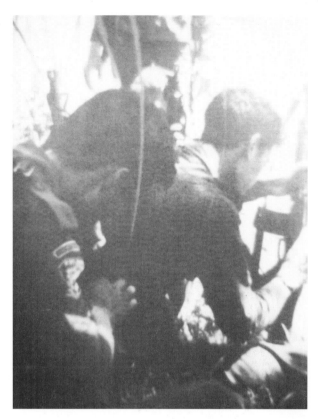

Blurred though it is, this shot of Malaysian commandos of the Special Services Regiment cleaning their weapons after an exercise does show the use of the commando shoulder title and patch, as in Plate J1a. (Official)

the unit was redesignated 1 Ranger Sdn., NZSAS in 1963. Between February 1965 and November 1966 four detachments (1–4 Det.) were rotated to Brunei during the Borneo confrontation. All parachute training was conducted in Australia until a jump school was opened in 1965 at an air force base at Whenuapai. In November 1968 4 Trp. NZSAS was sent to Vietnam, operating under the Australian SAS; two more troops, each designated 4 Trp., were to follow on one-year rotations until withdrawn in February 1971. On 1 April 1978 1 Ranger Sdn. was redesignated 1 NZSAS Sdn., at the same time the NZSAS Centre was established as a separate entity; both elements at Papakura Military Base. In 1983 Co. C, 21 Inf.Bn. was parachute qualified as a ready reaction force, and is located at Burnham Military Base near Christchurch.

Singapore

Formed in 1960, 1 Cdo.Bn's. training was initially conducted in the US with the entire unit taking the Airborne and Ranger Courses as well as other training. A jump school was established with New Zealand aid in 1970 as part of the Army School of Cdo. Training at Changi Air Base. Jungle training is sometimes conducted in Malaya. The school also runs a ranger course for the rest of the armed forces. Personnel completing their active duty are assigned to 10 Cdo.Bn. (Reserve).

Sri Lanka

In December 1977 a cadre was selected for a CT unit, and in February 1978 five volunteers were selected from each of the army's six battalions to undertake a selection course. In April

South Korean Special Forces pocket patches – see Plate I6. Blue oval grounds unless otherwise noted; black or white borders. (1) Special Warfare Centre: gold-yellow lion, black details, yellow ground. (2) 1st SF Bde.: gold eagle – a spread eagle variant exists. (3) 3rd SF Bde.: natural coloured tiger, gold mountains. (4) 5th SF Bde.: black dragon, red lightning, white parachute and details. (5) 7th SF Bde.: white horse. (6) 9th SF Bde.: orange 'ghost' face, red eyes and tongue, white parachute and whiskers, on black ground. (7) 11th SF Bde.: gold bat, red lightning, white detail, on black ground. (8) 13th SF Bde.: black leopard, white details. (C&D)

Two men of Singapore's 1st Commando Battalion, wearing the unit's bright red berets and camouflage uniforms. The weapon is the locally produced SAR80 assault rifle. (Singapore Defence Industries)

1978, 25 men from each battalion entered selection, and graduates were returned to their units. From October 1978 to April 1979 the graduates were returned in groups of 50 for advanced training. Of these 150 troops, 54 volunteered to join the new Cdo.Sdn. formed in April 1979 and based at Gemunu Watch at Diyatalawa. More volunteers were trained in 1980, and the unit moved to its present Ganamulla Base near Colombo. Twice a year volunteers attend a 35 day Basic Commando Selection Course. The roughly 40% who graduate attend a three-month Advanced Course. The unit began parachute training in India in December 1979. Due to political problems with India in 1982 jump training ceased, but the unit opened its own school at a later date. In March 1986 the 100-man squadron was enlarged to a regiment (bn.) due to the demands of the Tamil minority insurgency conducted by the 'Liberation Tigers of Tamil Eelam'.

Taiwan

The American OSS organised six company-sized **airborne** commando units within the Nationalist Chinese structure in 1945. These were to see action against the Japanese, with two of the units conducting combat jumps. In early 1946 these units were formed into a parachute corps and took part in ground action against the Chinese communists. After the Nationalist withdrawal to Taiwan a number of parachute, commando, and recon. units were formed; agents and sabotage teams were parachuted on to the mainland under CIA auspices. With the aid of USSF the Nationalists began to consolidate this mix of units into SF groups. The 1st SF Gp. was formed in January 1958, followed by the 2nd in March. More units were brought under the SF umbrella when the 3rd SF Gp. was activated in 1960 and the 4th in 1961. These units, under a combined SF HQ, are tasked with direct action, reconnaissance, and guerrilla activities. SF HQ also controls a number of company-sized commando units assigned specialised missions such as long-range amphibious reconnaissance and airmobile assault. The 1st and 2nd Abn. Battle Gps. (bdes.) were formed in the 1950s for conventional parachute operations.

Thai Special Forces senior NCOs demonstrate snake-handling during a survival class. Both wear a number of special skill badges, including foreign jump-wings; cf. Plate J6 (US Army)

Taiwan also maintains a 39,000-man **marine** corps with the 1st–3rd Marine Divs., support units, and 70,000 reserves. It was formed in 1949, and training assistance was provided by the US Marines in 1951. The corps HQ is located at Tsoying and the training centre at Fang-Shan.

Thailand

The first Thai SOF was the Royal Thai Army (RTA) Ranger Bn. (Abn.) formed at Lopburi in 1954 with USSF aid, beginning a long and close relationship. Though designated ranger, it was organised along the lines of a small USSF group. The RTA Special Warfare Centre was established at Ft. Narai, Lopburi in 1963 to both train and command SF units and to run the Ranger School. To co-ordinate the activities of the different units, both SF, conventional and police, the Communist Suppression Operations Command was formed in December 1965. This was immediately followed by a request for further assistance from the USSF, thus beginning the largest such operation outside Vietnam. The RTA Ranger Bn. had been redesignated the 1st SF Gp. in 1963; three of its detachments were paired up with USSF teams to form six joint detachments, three commanded by Thais. This joint effort was extremely successful, and it was not long before the RTA 2nd SF Gp. was formed. Though the USSF advisory effort ended in 1974, it was re-established in 1984. By 1982 there existed the 1st–4th SF Gps., which were redesignated regiments, and the 1st SF Div. was formed. In 1985, in response to the growing threat posed by Vietnamese forces in Kampuchea (formerly Cambodia), the 2nd SF Div. was formed and the 3rd SF Regt. assigned to it. The Special Warfare Command was also established in Bangkok to control both divisions plus LRRP units known as 'Tiger Scouts'. One such unit, 1st LRRP Trp., served in Vietnam with the RTA 'Black Panther' Expeditionary Div. in 1969–71. Today's RTA SF personnel are highly motivated and well trained. All must be parachute and ranger qualified before applying for SF training; there is a 60 per cent drop-out rate among applicants. The only conventional airborne unit is the 31st Abn.Regt., 1st Division.

A member of Thai Special Forces fully outfitted for a HALO jump. The Special Warfare Centre patch can be seen on his pocket – see Plate J6b. (Soldiers Magazine)

The Royal Thai **Marine** Corps (RTMC) dates from 1932, when a battalion was formed. Increased to a regiment in 1940, it battled communist insurgents both with the French in the 1950s and the US in the 1960s, when it was expanded to the RTMC Bde. with US Marine assistance. It also saw action on the Malayan border in the 1970s when it was again expanded into the 1st and 2nd RTMC Brigades. There are now 20,000 marines in the brigades' six infantry and one artillery regiments, and amphibious assault and recon. battalions.

Latin America

SOFs in this region are greatly influenced by the US through the efforts of USSF, mobile training teams (which have visited virtually every Latin American country), visiting officer training programmes at Ft. Benning, GA, and the School of the Americas.[1]

[1]The school was established in 1949 at Ft. Gurlich, Panama Canal Zone as the US Army Caribbean School. It was redesignated the School of the Americas in 1963 and relocated to Ft. Benning in 1984 when Ft. Gurlich was turned over to Panama. Its rôle is to train Latin American military personnel in advanced skills, new weapons, and CI. Spanish has been the exclusive language of instruction since 1956. It was locally supplemented by the Regional Military Training and Security Center established at Puerto Castilla, Honduras from 1983 to 1985.

Though of poor quality, this photograph is interesting in showing sergeants of the Guatemalan 1st Parachute Battalion, 1st Company relaxing in an NCOs' club. The size and position of insignia can be seen: cf. Plate K2. At this time the company patch was being worn on the left pocket and the patches of different platoons on the shoulder. Second and third from left wear the US Jungle Expert patch on their right pockets. (Official)

El Salvador

An army **airborne** company was formed in 1972 and enlarged to a battalion in 1974. It was under air force control until 1983, when it reverted to the army, and is based at Ilopango Airbase outside San Salvador along with the jump school. It was trained by USSF in a CI rôle and is now operating with one of the light infantry brigades. Also in 1972, the bn.-sized 1st and 2nd **Special Operations** Gps. (*1er y 2° Grupos Operacions Especiales*) were formed to combat increasing subversion. Advised by USSF, these units' activities are highly classified. The Special Operations School (*Escuela de Operacions Especiales*) is located at San Francisco Gotera. Guerrilla activities continued to increase, and the US poured in massive military aid beginning in 1979. The army, now enmeshed in a total civil war, began forming **ranger**-type CI light infantry battalions. The first three were raised in mid-1981 under the 4th Inf.Bde., to be followed in 1983 by a fourth. More have gradually been added and there are now 14 of these well-trained 1,000-plus man units.

In 1985 a new type of unit was formed to combat the infiltration of arms and supplies into El Salvador from Nicaragua, accomplished by boat across the Gulf de Fonseca. The navy formed two **naval infantry** battalions (*Batallón de Infanteria de Marina*) based at La Union and Usulatán. Formed from army infantrymen and naval commandos, they have proved to be fairly effective in executing interdiction and raid operations.

Guatemala

The Guatemalan jump school began operations in January 1961 at Retalhulev. The 1st Pcht.Plt. was formed at the same location in June. In June 1963 it was expanded to the 1st Pcht. Fusiliers Co. (*1er Companía de Paracaidistas de Fusilero*). The SF Co. (*Companía de Fuerza Especial*) was formed in December 1966

followed by the 2nd Pcht. Fusiliers Co. in mid-1970. The three units were consolidated as the 1st Parachute Bn. of the Army (*1er Batallón de Paracaidistas del Ejército*) on 1 January 1971 with the SF Co. becoming 3rd Co., and being based in San José. This unit is used to combat Cuban-backed guerrillas, an increasing problem since the late 1960s. USSF aid has been intermittent as US-Guatemalan relations see-sawed; most military assistance is now provided by Israel. Another CI unit also exists; although not parachute qualified, the **Tactical Security Gp.** of the Army (*Agrupacuón Táctica de Seguridad del Ejército*) is a highly trained reinforced battalion. Based in Guatemala City, it operates country-wide. The army has been relatively successful in combating the various insurgent groups, not only with CI operations, but also with a social development programme.

Honduras

Following the 1969 'Football War' with El Salvador the strength of the Honduran army was drastically increased, even though there is only an insignificant insurgency threat; the principal concerns are the occasional border incursions by Nicaragua and that country's massive military build-up. For this reason the army's organisation, based loosely on French principles, is aimed at a more conventional rôle rather than CI efforts. An **SF** unit of battalion size, simply the *Fuerza Especial*, was formed in 1973 with USSF assistance. Another airborne unit was formed in the late 1970s, but is under the Public Security Forces: the company-sized **Cobra Political Sdn.** (*Escuadron Policial Cobra*) increased to a battalion 1983. The 7th 'Venceremos' Inf.Bn. is reported to be an airborne, or at least an airmobile unit formed in the early 1980s. These units are served by a common parachute school (*Escuela de Paracaidismo*). The army also conducts a ranger course modelled after the US Army's, known as '*Teson*'.

Mexico

In 1933 a Mexican Army sergeant proposed the formation of a **parachute** trained 'air assault company', but the idea was rejected as there were no suitable aircraft. It was not until 1946, when a group of army and air force officers attended the US Parachute School that further efforts were made to form such a unit. The Small Air Troops Co. (*Mínimo Aerotropas Companía*) was formed at Puebla Pue as an element of the bde.-size

Honduran Special Forces major receiving roping instruction from a member of the US 193rd Infantry Brigade during an inter-allied jungle operations conference in Panama. The 'TESON' and Ranger tabs can be seen on the left shoulder above the unit patch – see Plate K3. (US Army)

Presidential Guard Corps. It was enlarged to a battalion in September 1952 and assigned to the air force. On 1 January 1969 the army formed the Pcht. Fusilier Bde. (*Brigada de Paracaidistas de Fusilero*) in Mexico City with two infantry and one training battalions (1st–3rd). The brigade's rôle is to act as a strategic reserve, and it is under the army general staff.

A non-airborne SPF unit, the **Assault Troops Bn**. (*Batallón de Tropas de Asalto*), formerly part of the Presidential Guard Corps, was re-assigned to the new Rapid Intervention Bde. (*Brigada de Intervencion Rápido*) along with two MP battalions in the mid-1980s. Based in Mexico City, the brigade is principally intended to respond to border crises with Guatemala and increasing insurgency in the south. It, too, is under the direct control of the general staff.

Nicaragua

Prior to the 1979 communist take-over the National Guard (army) had no SOF or SPF units. The victorious Sandinistas soon began a massive Soviet- and Cuban-backed military build-up. By 1985 the Sandinista Popular Army (*Ejercito Popular Sandinista*) had increased fourfold over the old National Guard, with 62,000 under arms. Build-up has continued, and strength now exceeds 77,000 active troops with even more reserves and militia as back-up. A Cuban-advised SOF **airborne** battalion was formed in 1982. Also trained for

Members of the Mexican Parachute Fusiliers Brigade. The parading soldiers wear helmet covers in the same colours and pattern as the US Army; the dark olive uniform has slanted flaps to the pleated pockets, and white metal snaps. The 1st Battalion patch is worn on the left shoulder. The two officers show the use of the brigade patch on the right shoulder; the parachute wings collar badges; and the rear box pleat and belt loops of the jacket. See Plate K6. The troops are armed with G3A3 rifles. (MSgt. Richard Dunlap)

airmobile operations, it has a direct action principal mission, but has also been used to combat the Contras. With the growth of the Contra movement and increased penetrations into Nicaragua, a new type of CI unit was formed: three '**irregular struggle battalions**' (*Batallón de Lucha Irregular*) were formed in 1983. These have been increased over the years, beginning in 1985, to 18 such units. Both Cubans and East Germans (probably Ministry for State Security) are known to advise these units.

Cuba

The pre-Castro Cuban Army formed a small **airborne** battalion in 1952, which was dissolved in 1959 along with the rest of the Constitutional Army. The Cuban exile landings during the ill-fated Bay of Pigs fiasco included a combat jump by Bde. 2506's 1st Bn. (co.). In the late 1960s the Ministry of the Revolutionary Armed Forces formed the brigade-sized Assault and Landing Troops (*Trupas de Asalto y Desembaco*); composed of two parachute and airmobile trained battalions, the unit is based in the Havana area and tasked as a rapid reaction force for the still-feared 'Yankee' invasion. Though it has not served

as a unit with Cuban expeditionary forces in Africa, small elements have. Advised by Soviets, its organisation and tactics are similar to those of the new Soviet air assault troops. Another SOF is the Havana based Ministry of Interior's Special Troops (*Trupas Especial*). Composed of two battalions with 1,500 troops, this force was formed in the mid-1960s, but was not publicly paraded until June 1976. Tasked with special direct action missions, it is thought to be advised by Soviet Spetsnaz officers. These were among the first troops sent to Angola in 1965 and elements are still committed there. These are also the troops thought to be involved in the attempted, and fatal, penetration of US Panama Canal bases in 1988.

The Revolutionary War Navy possesses a 550-man battalion-sized unit modelled after the Soviet **Naval Infantry**, the *Desembarco del Granma*. Formed in the late 1970s, it functions principally as a security force with only limited amphibious assault capability; however the navy did conduct its first significant amphibious exercise in 1983, employing this and army units.

Argentina

In 1947 the air force established a jump school at Córdoba and soon formed Pcht.Regt. 13, but under army control and attached to Inf.Div. 4. After the army formed its own **airborne** units, the air force unit was relegated to a secondary rôle and

Even this blurred picture shows that the black uniforms of the Cuban 'marines' are almost identical to those of their Soviet counterparts. (Official)

Shoulder patches of the Argentine Airborne Infantry Brigade IV. All have white borders and lettering, and gold devices. (1) IV Bde. HQ: blue background, gold 'IV' on green disc. (2) Abn. Inf. Regt. 2: green background. (3) Abn. Inf. Regts. 14 & 17: green background. (4) Abn. Arty. Group 4: red background. (5) Abn. Communications Co. 4: blue background. (6) Abn. Ordnance Co. 4: dark blue background.

reduced in size; today there is only a small SOF company. The army's first airborne unit was formed in 1952 with personnel training at the air force school, their first jump being made on 25 September 1952, considered the army airborne's formation date. The Army Paratroop School was formed in January 1954 taking over the facilities of the air force school.

The army undertook a major reorganisation in 1964 with brigades replacing the division as the principal tactical formation. Inf. Div. 4 provided the basis for Abn. Inf. Bde. IV (*Brigada de Infanteria Aerotransportada*), still based at Córdoba, under Army Corps 3. Bde. IV, formed on 16 November 1964, consists of: Abn. Inf. Regts. 2, 14 and 17 (bns.); Abn. Arty. Gp. 4 (bn.); and Abn. Communications and Ordnance Cos. 4. In the Argentine army most recruits undertake basic training within their units. Airborne troops receive theirs in Abn. Tng. Regt. 13 (bn.) at Mendoza—thus permitting Bde. IV to maintain a high degree of readiness—followed by the Abn. Forces School at Córdoba. Some Bde. IV personnel receive additional training at the Jungle Warfare School at Corrientes and the Mountain Warfare School at Mendoza, which also trains VII Jungle and V, VI and VIII Mountain Inf. Bdes. Bde. IV also conducts airmobile training. The only Bde. IV element to see combat in the Falklands was Abn. Inf. Regt. 2, which fought Britain's 2 Para at Goose Green before surrendering.

Two small **commando** units also fought in the Falklands; Cdo.Cos. 601 and 602 (*Companía de Comando*), both hurriedly formed from elements of SF Gp. 601 (bn.) and recalled commando-trained personnel. This system proved disastrous as the troops had not trained as a unit, and lacked cohesion and current proficiency.[1] Commando training is carried out at the commando branch of the School of Infantry at Campo de Mayo, Buenos Aires. Begun in 1964, it was modelled after the US Ranger Course until 1967, when it was superceded by a CI course; re-established in 1968, the commando course now included CI instruction. SF Gp. 601 (*Grupa de Fuerzas Especiales*)

[1]See Argentine Army Commandos in the Falklands, 1982, *Military Illustrated Past & Present* No. 3, 1986.

itself was formed in the late 1960s and based at Palomar Barracks, Buenos Aires.

The *Infantería de Marina* traces its history to an ad hoc naval artillery battalion which resisted the failed British invasion of 1807; an actual **marine** unit was not formed until 1827, however. Name and rôle changes, inactivations and re-activations were frequently inflicted on the marines, until they were finally made a separate naval branch in 1968. A coast defence and security force until reorganised as an amphibious unit in 1949, the marine infantry continued to grow, receiving aid from the US Marines. Elements of Marine Inf. Bde. 1, including a special commando unit, '*Buzos Tacticos*', provided the initial Falklands invasion force, most being withdrawn and replaced by lower quality army units.[1] Today's marines consist of about 6,000 troops organised into Marine Force 1, headquartered in Buenos Aires with Marine Inf. Regt. 1 composed of Inf. Bns. 3 and 5; and Marine Force 2, headquartered at Baterias. This latter controls the main strike force, Marine Inf. Bde. 1, with:

Marine Inf.Bns. 1 & 2	Anti-Aircraft Arty.Regt. 1
Amph.Cdo.Gp. (bn.)[2]	AT, Mortar, & Engineer
Arty., Amph. Vehicle, &	Cos. 1
Comm. Bns. 1	

Separate units include Inf.Bn. 4, Marine Service Bn., and Security Cos. 1 & 4–8.

Bolivia

In 1960 the Bolivian Army formed the Special Troops Instruction Centre (*Centro de Instrucción de Tropas Especiales*) and a small experimental **parachute** battalion at Cohabanba with USSF aid. The battalion was subsequently enlarged and participated in some CI operations during Ernesto 'Ché' Guevara's unsuccessful attempt to introduce a Cuban-style revolution. The Pcht.Bn., still at Cohabanba, is subordinate to the 7th Division. The 1960s emphasis on CI caused the air force to form air units to support this mission along with the 'Americus' Pcht.Bn. in 1967. Advanced training is given to some paratroopers, including a freefall course, which results in the award of the Jump Commando (*Salto Comando*) badge.

The USSF also assisted with the formation of a Ranger School near Santa Cruz in 1967. Here three battalions of Andean Indians were trained specifically to hunt down Ché Guevara's guerrilla band, which had proved difficult for conventional units. The 2nd Ranger Bn. was successful in October 1967 when the band was wiped out; it is rumoured that USSF personnel directly participated. The army was reorganised in the early 1970s, and the three ranger battalions were absorbed into two existing infantry regiments to help convert these to ranger status. The 12th 'Manchego' Ranger Regt. is under the 8th Div. at Santa Cruz and the 24th 'Mindez Arcos' Ranger Regt. is under the 2nd Div. at Challapata, each with two battalions. The rangers also undertake jungle and mountain training along with the 5th 'Lanza', 17th 'Illimani' and 19th 'Murillo' Andean (mountain) Regts.

Brazil

Brazil sent a small number of officers and NCOs to the US Parachute School in 1945. They soon established their own school in Rio de Janeiro to train the new Parachute Bde.

[1]See MAA 133, *Battle for The Falklands (1) Land Forces*.
[2]Formed from the Marine Amph. Cdo. Co., they are variously known as *Buzos Tacticos* (Tactical Divers), *Comandos Amfibios* (Amph.Cdos.), and *Infanparacaibuzos* (Inf.Para Divers).

Brazilian paratroopers, wearing maroon berets with a parachute badge, 'duck hunter' camouflage, and armed with FAL rifles, mounted in a locally-made SAFO-1 light air-droppable vehicle. (Official)

formed in 1946. Later a cadre Abn.Div. HQ was formed for future expansion of the **parachute** force. The brigade formed a small para-rescue unit in 1957; its mission and size expanded, and it was designated the SF Bn. in 1983. The Pcht.Bde. had '1st' added to its designation in the mid-1970s when the 2nd Pcht.Bde. was formed at Brasília; each brigade had three battalions. The Abn.Div. HQ has apparently disbanded; the 1st Bde. is under 1st Army HQ and the 2nd subordinate to 5th Army.

Brazil's vast Amazon basin, with its lush rain forests and extensive river systems, requires special training for soldiers and units to operate there effectively. The country's attempts to develop this region and potential troubles with northern neighbours led to increased military interest in this environment. The Jungle Warfare Instruction Centre (*Centro de Instrucao de Guerra na Selva*) was formed at Manaue in 1964, modelled after the US Jungle Warfare Centre in Panama but modified to meet the unique demands of the Amazon region. It was later redesignated the Jungle and Cdo. Action Operations Centre (*Centro de Operacoes na Selva e Accoeo de Comandoes*). It offers several courses including an 11-week commando course conducted entirely in Brazil's jungles, mountains, semi-desert areas and sea coasts. Three Jungle Operations Courses include: Stage A—teaches senior officers how to operate units in the jungle in five weeks; Stage B—teaches junior officers to lead companies in the jungle in six weeks, Stage C—trains NCOs to

lead platoons and squads in five weeks. In the mid-1970s the 1st–5th Jungle Warfare Bns. were formed and stationed in the Amazon basin subordinate to the Amazon Military Command headquartered in Manaus.

The Brazilian **marines** attribute their origins to the Portuguese Royal Naval Brigade. The Corps considers its founding date as 7 March 1808, when the brigade arrived in Brazil escorting the royal family fleeing Napoleon's invasion. One of its battalions remained when the royal family returned home in 1821. Many title changes later it was to receive its present designation in 1932, Corps of Naval Fusiliers (*Corpo de Fuzileiros Navais*), which it had also borne from 1846 to 1852. Involved in all of Brazil's wars through the 1800s, the *Fuzileiros Navais* expected to be sent overseas when war was declared on Germany in 1942, but this honour went to the army. (The Expeditionary Div. fought with distinction under US command in Italy, while the marines performed only home coastal security duties.) In 1965 the marines were finally sent outside their country in support of the Organisation of American States' intervention in the Dominican Republic; there they served alongside US Marines and the relationship has continued. Today's *Fuzileiros Navais* consists of about 14,500 troops with headquarters at Ft. São José, Rio de Janeiro. Also headquartered there is the Fleet Marine Force consisting of the 1st Amph.Div. (*Divisáo Anfibia*): Inf.Bns. 1st 'Riachuelo', 2nd 'Humaita' and 3rd 'Paissandú'; Arty.Gp.; and 1st Engineer and 1st Service Battalions. Force Troops include Special Operations Bn. 'Toneleros', service units, and ships detachments, the former originally formed in 1957 as a parachute qualified, company-sized SEAL-type unit.

Brazilian paratroopers carry the body of a prospector killed by Indians to a helicopter pick-up zone. Their duties have often involved such tasks. Their uniforms in this case are similar to US jungle fatigues. (Official)

Company-sized security units, which guard naval bases and off-shore islands, consist of Regional Gps. I–VII and Security Gps. I and II.

Colombia

Colombia became the first Latin American country to form an SOF unit. The School of Lancers (*Escuela de Lanceros*) was established at Tolemaida in 1955 and modelled after the US Army's Ranger Course, but with special emphasis on CI. The Bn. of Lancers (*Batallón de Lanceros*) was soon formed with a ranger/CI mission; its personnel are also airborne qualified.

In 1946–57 a virtual civil war, known as '*La Violencia*', caused the formation of even earlier CI units, Bdes. VII and VIII. Unlike conventional brigades with a full combined arms complement, these units have only one service and two infantry battalions. Two more, IX and X, were formed in 1974. The Airborne Bn. (*Batallón Aerotransportado*) was formed at Villavicencio in March 1964. Many of these units' officers and NCOs attend the Lancero School. The ten-week course is divided into three phases, each progressively more demanding in leadership and individual combat skills.

The exact year of the founding of the Corps of **Naval Infantry** (*Cuerpo de Navais Infantaria*) is lost in history, but was around 1810. Disbanded in 1845 along with the rest of the navy, it was re-formed with that service's reappearance in 1907. Colombia conducted as amphibious operation during the 1932–33 Leticia War with Peru: three river gunboats, purchased from Britain, crossed the Atlantic on their own to rendezvous with another and landed 1,000 naval infantry, navy, and army troops who succeeded in driving the invaders from the disputed area. The naval infantry reorganised in 1936 into two companies, expanding to a battalion in 1940. Volunteer officers and NCOs accompanied *1er Batallon Colombia* (an army unit) to Korea in 1951–54, Colombia being the only Latin American country to contribute forces to the UN. The 1,500-man naval infantry consists of the 1st and 2nd Bns. at Cartagena and Buenaventura respectively, three security companies, naval police, and a small airborne commando unit. Training is conducted at Cartagena.

Ecuador

A jump school was established in 1958 with US assistance and a small **parachute** battalion formed the following year at Quito. That same year a cadre of officers and NCOs attended the US Ranger Course and returned to establish a similar one. An army frogman course was begun in 1958. In 1960 these three special operations disciplines were combined to form the battalion-sized Special Parachutist Det. (*Destacamento Especial de Paracaidistas*). By 1962 the unit was conducting CI operations in eastern Ecuador. In 1964 a battalion-sized, airborne trained SF Jungle Det. was formed at San Camilo, to augment the counter-guerrilla effort. In 1975 these two units were consolidated into the Pcht.Bde., later redesignated 1st 'Patria' SF Bde. and under Army HQ control. Headquartered at Quito, the Para Det. became the 1st SF Gp. (bn.), also at Quito, and the Jungle Det. became the 2nd SF Gp. remaining at San Camilo. The jump and SF schools are located in Salinas. The jungle school, where SF and jungle unit personnel are trained, is located 'somewhere in the eastern jungles'. The **jungle brigades**, containing two battalions tasked with a CI rôle, are the 19th 'Napo' under 1st Army Div. and 68th 'Pastaza' under the 6th Army Div.

The most recently established Latin American **marine** corps was unofficially formed on 25 July 1962 after the navy procured its first landing craft. This amphibious battalion was officially recognised on 12 November 1966 with the formation of a security battalion. The 700-man plus Navy Infantry Corps (*Cuerpo de Infanteria de Marina*), headquartered in Guayaquil, is now organised into two security battalions, one operating on the many small eastern rivers and the other at Pacific coast navy bases. The commando battalion in the Galápagos Islands has both amphibious warfare and security duties.

Venezuela

Venezuela formed the 1st and 2nd Abn.Bns. (*Batallónes Aerotransportada*) with US assistance in the mid-1950s, during an expansion of the armed forces. In the late 1970s they were consolidated with the air force's **airborne** battalion, formed in the late 1950s, to form Abn.Gp. 'Aragua' (*Agrupación Aerotransportada*). All elements are based at Maracay along with the airborne school. The group is subordinate to the air force, but under the control of the Joint Staff of the Armed Forces. Group personnel are provided by the army and air force, with most officers from the army; all personnel wear air force uniform.

An airborne Cdo.Bn. (*Battallóne de Comandos*) was formed in the early 1960s as a CI effort. Parachute delivery of its subunits proved extremely difficult in the mountainous jungle terrain and it was soon disbanded. It was replaced by non-airborne 'hunter' battalions (*Batallónes de Cazadores*): light infantry **ranger**-type units, of which 13 were formed in the late 1960s and early 1970s. CI efforts were largely successful, and four of the battalions are now consolidated in a 'hunter' brigade along with two conventional infantry battalions; the other battalions are assigned three each to the 1st, 2nd, and 3rd Divs. in northern and north-western Venezuela.

The combined **marine** corps of the Republic of Gran Colombia (Colombian, Equadorian and Venezuelan confederation) were principally provided by the latter. Formed in 1822, they were dissolved in 1829, and were not re-established until 1 July 1938, when a company was formed to provide ships' detachments. A second company was formed on 8 December 1939 and a third on 9 September 1943. They were consolidated into the 1st Naval Inf.Bn. (*Battallóne de Infanteria de Marina—BIM*) on 11 December 1945, now the anniversary of the Naval Infantry Corps, and based at Puerto Cabello. In February 1946 the 2nd BIM was formed at the same location and the 1st relocated to Marquetia. Naval Infantry HQ was located at Caracas. The 3rd BIM was organised at Carupano in 1958 with the acquisition of additional landing craft. In June 1962 the 2nd BIM staged a mutiny, suppressed by the navy and other naval infantry. The 4th BIM was organised in the mid-1980s, and a number of support units had been formed over the years. Current units contain 5,200 troops:

1st BIM 'Simon Bolivar'	Amph. Assault Bn.
2nd BIM 'General Rafael Urdaneta'	Naval Police Regt.
3rd BIM 'Mariscal Antonio Jose de Sucre'	Two small para-commando units
4th BIM 'Francisco de Miranda'	Engineer, signal, transport, & river patrol units
Arty.Bn. (1 air defence & 3 howitzer btys.)	

The formation of a light tank battalion is projected in the near future.

The Plates

A1: Belgium: Caporal-chef 2 (Commando) Battalion, Para-Commando Regiment
The regiment's 2 and 4 (Cdo.) Bns., Arty.Bty. and AT Co. wear the green beret inherited from the British Commandos; both battalions wear this cap badge (1a), while other regimental units use a silver badge similar to that of the British Parachute Regt. but lacking the lion and crown, and with a dagger superimposed, upwards, on the parachute. (Inset 1b) Commando 'B' qualification badge, worn on service dress, left forearm.

A2: Belgium: Sous-lieutenant, 1 Special Recon. Teams Company, Para-Commando Regiment
The maroon beret is worn by 1 and 3 (Para) Bns., the Recon.Sdn. and the 1 *ESR* Company. Between 1955 (when the battalion was formed in the Congo with men from both 1 and 2 Bns.) and 1959, 3 Bn. wore brown berets with the badge of the Korean War *Battalion Belge*, as shown at (2b)—now worn on the maroon beret. 1 *ESR* Co. and 1 (Para) Bn. now share the badge shown at (2a). Both A1 and A2 wear Belgian camouflage uniforms, with rank on shoulder slides in unit colours.

A3: France: Soldat de 1ere classe, 13e Régiment de Dragons Parachutistes
The 'maroon' beret—in practice, often nearer dark scarlet—has been worn by all French *paras* apart from the *légionnaires* of the REPs since September 1957, with the cap badge of the *Troupes Aeroportées* (3a) for all except Colonial/Marine units. Standard para-wings brevet, and the enamelled regimental badge, are worn above and below the velcro'd name tape; the velcro'd chest patch bears the diagonal rank stripe. The uniform is the universal 'army green' *tenue de combat mle 1964*, worn by this LRRP over the zipped winter cardigan.

A4: France: Caporal-chef, 2e Régiment Parachutiste d'Infanterie de Marine
The Colonial/Marine *paras* have always worn the red beret, with this badge (4a) incorporating the TAP and Colonial motifs in 1958–62 and again since 1974; in the interim they wore a gold version in a ring. For tropical tours of duty French troops are issued an updated version of the *tenue de combat camouflée de toutes armes mle 1947*. Rank is worn in the colour and 'metal' of the branch—red and gold for Marine troops. (Inset 4b) The Commando Training Centres badge design, here with 'R' for 'Réunion'.

A5: France: Sergent-chef, 27e Bataillon de Chasseurs Alpins
The large Basque beret has been worn by the Alpine Light Infantry since 1889, a year after the branch was raised from the *Chasseurs à pied*—from whom the hunting-horn badge was also taken. The unit and branch *ecusson* (5a) is worn on the left sleeve of service dress. The camouflage smock shown is in the commercial 'K-Way/Salik International' pattern acquired semi-officially by some French units.

A6: France: Quartier-maitre de 1ere classe, Groupement de Fusiliers-Marins Commandos
This naval commando unit is unique in the French forces in wearing the beret pulled right in commemoration of wartime attachment to the British Commandos; the bronze cap badge (6a) dates from the same period, as does the manner of wearing naval rank on shoulder strap slides. The smock seen here is the old *mle 1947/56 veste de saut camouflée*, withdrawn from use by the *paras* in 1963. Depending on the model of service uniform and the rank, this unit wears 'COMMANDO' shoulder titles in red or gold on black and blue on white. (Inset 6b) Combat swimmer brevet.

B1: Netherlands: Korporaal, 104 Waarnemings- en Verkennings-compagnie
The green beret and badge (1a) are worn by both 104 Recon. & Surveillance Co. and 35 Commando Battalion; the original Special Troops Regt. wore maroon, but green berets have been awarded by the Assault School since 1945. (Inset 1b) Title and patch worn on left shoulder of service dress.

B2: Netherlands: Sekondlojtnant, Koninklijk Nederlands Korps Mariniers
This officer of the 1 Amphibious Combat Group wears no insignia on his British DPM smock, issued because his unit is closely aligned for training, and wartime mission, with Britain's 3 Cdo.Bde., Royal Marines. The badge and backing (2a) are common throughout the KNKM; the title (2b) is worn on the left shoulder of service dress.

B3: Federal Germany: Stabsunteroffizier, 300.Fernspähkompanie
Only limited use is now made of camouflage clothing in the German forces, although they were pioneers in this field. The maroon beret was adopted for all airborne units in the early 1960s. The badge (3a) includes lances, which with the gold-yellow *Waffenfarbe* shoulder strap loops indicate the LRRP companies' cavalry lineage. The similar beret badge of 1 Air Landing Div. has a slightly differently posed eagle and lacks the lances and lightnings. These LRRP companies wear, on service dress, the left shoulder patch of the parent Corps—e.g. (3b). The *Einzelkämpfer* or Close Combatant badge (3c), worn on the right breast pocket of service dress, is sometimes incorrectly termed a 'ranger' badge.

B4: Federal Germany: Obergefreiter, 23.Gebirgsjägerbrigade
The 1 Mountain Div. refused the dark green *Jäger* beret when offered in in 1971, preferring the traditional *Bergmütze* derived from a pre-1914 Austrian design. The traditional edelweiss badge, worn by German mountain troops since World War I, is retained on the cap side and in the brigade's service dress shoulder patch (4a), and the Army Mountain Leader badge (4b) worn on the right pocket. Divisional troops wear the same design of patch as (4a) but with different edging: silver (Div. elements), white (*22.Panzergrenadierbrigade*), red (*23.Gebirgsjäger-brigade*) and yellow (*24.Panzerbrigade*).

B5: Switzerland: Korporal, Fernspäh-Kompanie 17
This highly selective unit wears no special beret or insignia other than the jump-wings: however, the rank slide—normally worn on the right only—may be of a unit-specific colour combination. This jumper is wearing a leather protective helmet, and the standard Swiss army camouflage smock, notable for its many pockets and integral buckles and clips for attachment of equipment, and for the strong red tinge of elements of the pattern.

B6: Canada: Sergeant, Canadian Airborne Regiment
This NCO serving with the Special Service Force wears the standard Mk II field uniform; the British DPM smock is worn in the field. The maroon beret bears the CAR badge (6a) in all three Airborne Commandos, and the SSF cap badge (6b) in Force HQ. Note SSF shoulder patch; unit-specific national title on strap slide, incorporating jump-wings; and jump-wings with white maple leaf marking assignment to an airborne unit—a red leaf means non-jump status. Most field insignia are in tan on olive.

C1: Finland: Vaapeli, Coastal Ranger Battalion
The green beret denotes the unit's commando rôle; the collar patches display rank on a background of the traditional *jaeger* colour. (Inset 1a) Beret badge.

C2: Finland: Alikersantti, Airborne Jaeger School
The school cadre of the LJK wear the maroon beret with the badge (2a); graduates are awarded it, but may not wear it after

Oberfeldwebel of Federal German paratroops in shirtsleeve barracks dress with insignia, 1984. Rank—dull light grey shoulder strap braid outline, enclosing two chevrons—is indicated on the shoulder strap slides, which have the grass green outer loop worn by all infantry including airborne. He wears the maroon beret with wreathed diving eagle badge; national flashes on both upper sleeves; cloth versions of German above French jump-wings, both in white and yellow on pale drab backing; full-colour cloth Close Combatant badge; and nametape, above an unidentified badge. (Brian Leigh Davis)

returning to their units. Ranking is worn on OD patches on the collar of the camouflage uniform.

C3: Denmark: Oversergent, Jaeger Corps
The beret badge (3a) of the *Jaegerkorpset* links today's unit with the heraldry of the original 18th-century corps. The uniform is the new m/85 camouflage clothing. The 'JAEGER' title (3b) is worn by those passing Selection 2; the 'PATRULJE' title by graduates of the Patrolling Course, both on the left shoulder of service uniform. There was a silver-on-green 'PATRULJE' title for the four-week *Patrulje 1* course, but this was eliminated when the courses were combined in 1981–82.

C4: Sweden: Fanjunkare, Lapland Jaeger Regiment (I22)
The green beret is worn as a mark of the ranger rôle by all three *Jägare* units. I22's beret badge follows the design of the unit's left shoulder patch for service dress—the wolf's head is referred to by members of the Northlands Dragoon Regt. as 'an angry poodle on a fried egg'. The shoulder titles worn by the

Northlands Dragons (K4) and Life Hussars (K3)—illustrated as insets (4b) and (4c)—are considered by men of I22 to be 'so uninteresting as not to warrant comment! This spotted camouflage uniform, reminiscent of the World War II SS pattern, was an experimental type not finally selected; a splinter pattern is worn instead.

C5: Sweden: Kapten, Army Parachute-Jaeger School
The symbol of the *Armáns-fallskarmjägerskola*, which school personnel refer to as the 'ice-cream cone', is worn both as a beret badge (5a) and service dress shoulder patch (5b). This instructor officer wears the new m/87 sweater with shoulder strap slide ranking.

C6: Sweden: Private, Coastal Jaeger School, Waxholm Coastal Artillery Regiment 1
'Neptune's trident' is worn as the beret badge in three unofficial variants: straight tangs, as here, by the standard 'amphibious rangers'; with tines bent inwards (6a) by 'attack divers'; and angled on the beret, with the tines higher, by the sea transport unit. The 'KUSTJÄGARNA' title is awarded on course graduation, and is worn beneath the shoulder patch of the parent Waxholm Regiment (6b). The field collar patches on the m/59 uniform (the same cut as the m/58, which was grey) are in OD with light OG edges and embroidered yellow infantry symbols.

D1: Norway: Sersjant, Jaeger School
The national cap badge (1a) is worn on the *Jeger's* maroon beret; the national flash on the left sleeve of the camouflage jacket, recently issued to conventional units as well.

D2: Norway: Menig 1 Saerklasse, Naval Jaeger Company
The beret, flash and badge (2a) are worn by all Norwegian Navy personnel. The two Naval Jaeger Companies at Ramsund, whose patch is worn on the left shoulder, enjoy much latitude in field uniform choice: this man wears a US jungle fatigue shirt under his issue field jacket.

D3: Italy: Caporale Maggiore, 9th Parachute Raider Battalion 'Colonel Moschin'
A common beret badge with a unit number disc is worn by most 'Folgore' Parachute Brigade units; unnumbered units wear the version at (3a). An OD-khaki beret was used 1948–60; then a grey-green beret, until maroon was adopted in 1968. The current service dress left shoulder patch, with lightning (3b), was adopted in 1967 when the 'Folgore' title was awarded. The uniform is a special padded version, in a camouflage pattern used more or less unchanged since World War II. The jacket bears the Italian national collar stars used since 1871; left chest ranking; and a name-tape, to which, interestingly, the individual's blood group has been added. The School of Military Parachuting uses the old shoulder patch, as (3b) but without lightning, with a black-on-white title 'SC.MIL. PARACADUTISMO'.

D4: Italy: Soldato, Alpine Brigade 'Tridentina'
The traditional Alpine hat, introduced originally in black leather before World War I, has an eagle feather (pre-dating the hat) in a company-coloured wool holder, and the *Alpini* branch cap badge (4a). National collar stars and left arm flash are applied to an insulated Alpine parka. The parachute platoons of the five Alpine brigades and the para-company of IV Alpine Corps all wear this same hat.

D5: Italy: Caporale, Marine Battalion 'San Marco'
The black beret and badge (5a) date from the re-activation of 1965, and are influenced by the Army's 'Lagunari'. The cuff insignia of the unit, seen here on the one-piece camouflage uniform, is not worn in the field. The national flash is of the type worn by the unit in Lebanon, 1983, and contrasts with the Army's simpler flash.

D6: Greece: Epilochias, Special Raider Force Battalion
The 1976 standard Greek Army badge is seen here on the green beret worn by para, commando and SRF battalions of the Para-Commando Division; the Marines wear it on dark blue berets. The shoulder patch (6a) and title are also common to non-Marine units of the division; the patch worn by 32nd Marine Infantry Regiment is inset (6b). Note yellow-on-grass green ranking on left collar; and grass and lime green subdued version of master parachutist's wings on left breast.

E1: Spain: Brigada, 2nd Parachute Battalion 'Roger de Lauria'
Both this standard issue OD fatigue uniform, and locally made camouflage uniforms resembling US BDU pattern, are worn at various times by Spanish airborne units. On the former, but not the latter, the higher formation sign (here the Para Bde.) is worn in subdued form on the upper right sleeve, and a battalion patch on the left. This warrant officer's rank is worn in gold and red to the right of the airborne troops' cap badge (inset 1a) and on the left breast.

E2: Spain: Guerillero, 101 Special Operations Company
The distinctive green, white, brown and dark brown mottled camouflage uniform—one of several variants—is associated with the SO Groups. No insignia are worn other than the subdued jump-wings, and the plain green shoulder strap slide of these units. The badge of this branch is worn on a dark green beret (2a). (Inset 2b) Group patch, worn on the left shoulder of service dress; the design appears in different colour combinations according to unit.

E3: Portugal: Segundo Furriel, Commando Regiment
The regiment's maroon beret, and distinctive cap badge, are a carry-over from the commando companies which served in Portuguese colonial campaigns in Africa. Camouflage uniforms, of various slightly differing types, have been based on French models since 1960. Rank is worn on shoulder strap slides. The 'COMANDO' title (3a) is worn on the left shoulder of service dress. Parachute troops wear a dark green beret, marines black, each with their own insignia.

E4: Yugoslavia: Desetar, 36th Parachute Brigade
The standard army uniform is worn, with the brigade patch (4a) on both upper sleeves; ranking on the shoulder straps; and the brigade's OD beret with special enamelled badge. This unit does not wear the parachutist's badge—similar to the Soviet model—on the everyday uniform.

E5: Iraq: 'Arif, 66th Commando Brigade
Iraqi uniforms are almost devoid of insignia. The cap badge worn here—horizontal gold sword below red disc on white, all in gold wreath—is worn by all army elements.

E6: Iran: Goruhban Dovon, Special Forces Division
Fundamentalist Iran has retained many of the insignia of the Shah's regime, including US-style enlisted rank insignia. The jump-wings have lost the gold crown which surmounted the

parachute before the revolution. Several similar styles of cap badge (inset 6a) have been observed. A rag-tag collection of camouflage uniforms of different origins is now in use. The 'COMMANDO' title is worn on service dress; note that the script is in both Farsi and English (6b).

F1: Jordan: Raquib, Special Forces Brigade

The paratroopers' maroon beret bears the national cap badge (1a). Until recent years the formation wore a mixture of British-, Egyptian- and Romanian-made camouflage uniforms as the Jordanian government bought bulk supplies according to the best available deals; now, however, US-style BDU is the norm. Rank is worn on both sleeves of most Jordanian field uniforms. The advanced parachutists's wings are worn on his left breast, the plastic free-fall parachutist's badge on the right. On service dress the 'Ranger' title and Special Forces patch (1b) are worn on both sleeves.

F2: Oman: Raqib Awwal, Sultan's Special Force

This hand-picked battalion is advised by the British SAS, and wears an obvious copy of their cap badge, with Arabic script, on the royal purple beret adopted when the Sultan became the nominal commander (an orange beret was previously worn). On this recently adopted desert camouflage uniform ranking and yellow-on-purple abbreviated titles are worn on sand-coloured shoulder strap slides; a unit lanyard on the left shoulder; and the unit's special jump-wings, with crown and sceptres, on the right breast. (Inset 2a) The plainer jump-wings worn by the Parachute Regiment.

F3: Saudi Arabia: Raqib Awwal, Airborne Brigade

The national cap badge is worn on the maroon beret. The desert camouflage uniform adopted in the 1970s bears ranking below a 'Ranger' title on the sleeve, and metal jump-wings.

F4: Syria: Musa'id, Commando Brigade

In the past the Syrians appear to have had a different camouflage uniform for every day of the week . . . this 'vertical lizard' pattern was common among SOFs; but recently they seem to have settled on one similar to US BDU. The exact organisational chart of the many small units of paratroops and commandos is confused, but all now seem to be concentrated into a Special Forces Division. The maroon beret seems to indicate airborne status in both types of unit; the badge (4a) is the national pattern. The different commando groups wear the skull-and-swords design as a cloth patch and as a left breast badge on service dress (4b), the backing colour differing with the unit. Below the patch is worn the rank insignia of a junior warrant officer, on green infantry branch backing. (Insets 4c, 4d) Airborne Brigade and Commando Brigade plastic patches.

F5: Turkey: Astegmen, Para-Commando Brigade

The recently introduced light blue beret of airborne troops bears the officers'-pattern national badge (5a) on a green (infantry) backing; NCOs' badges have no wreath, and enlisted men wear no badge. The rank of acting second lieutenant, in subdued form, is worn on the shoulder straps of the indigenous camouflage uniform peculiar to airborne formations. The para-commando patch on the breast doubles as jump-wings and commando qualification insignia; there are several variants, one inscribed 'KOMANDO'. On service dress the Para-Cdo.Bde. patch (5b) is worn on the left shoulder, the metal version of the wings/qualification badge (5c) on the breast.

F6: Turkey: Onbasi, Amphibious Infantry Brigade

This locally-made uniform in US BDU pattern is worn only by the Amph.Inf.Bde., whose rank insignia are in red for conscript personnel; the subdued left breast insignia (6a) is that of the brigade, and appears on both OD and camouflage backings.

G1: North Yemen: Raqib Awwal, 'Al Mithalaat' Brigade

The badge (1a) on the maroon beret is that worn by all N. Yemeni forces. The beret itself was distinctive of the paratroops and SF until 1985, when maroon was adopted by all army personnel—much to the fury of its previous wearers. Insignia styles are very Egyptian—indeed, the paratroops' badge worn beside the jump-wings on the left breast is identical to the Egyptian type (inset 3b). (Inset 1b) Commando badge.

G2: Djibouti: Soldat, Parachute Company

Trained and equipped by the French, who supplied the red berets and 1947 general service camouflage uniforms, this company has a distinctive beret badge (2a), and wears its enamelled unit badge on a chest fob in the French manner: blue

Hauptfeldwebel of the 26 Air-Landing Brigade, 1st Air-Landing Division, Federal German Army in walking-out uniform, 1984. The silver paratrooper's badge on the maroon beret is clearly seen. White shirt and black tie are worn with the light grey M1957 tunic; collar and shoulder straps are piped and braided gold; the silver collar patches have green backing, the shoulder straps green outer piping; the red edge of the left sleeve patch identifies the brigade within the division—bright blue, silver parachute motif. (Brian Leigh Davis)

shield, red edge with gold script, gold diving eagle superimposed on white parachute, all over red star.

G3: Egypt: 'Arif, 182nd Parachute Brigade
The cap badge (3a) is common throughout the Egyptian armed forces, though it appears in officers' and enlisted men's versions. The reversible camouflage uniform bears shoulder slide ranking and silver jump-wings. The paratroopers' shoulder title and patch (3b) are worn on the left sleeve of service uniform, and the smaller enamelled version of the patch (illustrated) is sometimes seen on the left chest.

G4: Egypt: Mulazim Awwal, 127th Commando Group
The same uniform as G3, reversed, worn here with the commandos' black beret. (Inset 4a) Equivalent title and badge of commandos, worn in same way as paratroop insignia.

G5: Libya: Mulazim, Commando-Parachute Brigade
The cap badge (5a) is apparently worn by most Libyan armed forces, but here on the distinctive blue beret. In most countries the interlocked ring motif on jump-wings signifies an instructor, but they are present on all grades of Libyan wings. The unit patch (5b) is worn high on both sleeves, the eagle's head to the front on both sides.

G6: Morocco: Parachute Brigade
The French influence is very clear. All personnel of most army branches wear the dark green beret with service dress, though not with the OG field uniform. The national badge (6b) varies with rank: small gold wreath, enlisted ranks; small silver wreath, NCOs; large gold wreath, subaltern officers; large silver wreath, field officers. The tan service tunic has light grey semi-rigid shoulder boards, and winged parachute collar badges. (Inset 6a) Left sleeve insignia of unit and rank; in the French manner, this is worn with chevrons and braid of different types by different ranks. Again in French style, the unit badge is worn on a chest fob in enamels—silver crowned wreath and parachute, the shrouds terminating in a star, on maroon background.

H1: Somalia: 6th Commando Regiment
Apart from his jump-wings, this wadaddo (warrior) wears no distinctive unit insignia.

H2: Sudan: Mulazim Awwal, 144th Parachute Brigade
For some reason this officer wears an enlisted man's version of the unit cap badge; the correct officers' version is inset (2a). The unit patch (2b) is plastic-covered. The eagle motif on the jump-wings and officer's cap badge replaced a rhinoceros as the national symbol in 1972.

H3: Angola: Soldado, Parachute Battalion
Both the beret badge (3a) and jump-wings were adopted after the MPLA government gained power from the Portuguese and the rival FNLA.

H4: Kenya: Second Lieutenant, Parachute Battalion
The uniform is entirely British in style, and British DPM uniform is worn in the field.

H5: South Africa: Onder Korporaal, 44 Parachute Brigade
The paratroopers' cap badge (5a) is worn on a beret slightly lighter in tone than British maroon. The brigade patch and bar are worn on the left sleeve of the bush-brown shirt; camouflage

uniform has been introduced for field use. (Inset 5b) 2 Para Bn. badge; since 1 Para Bn. is not subordinate to 44 Bde., it has its own unique badge design (5c).

H6: Zimbabwe: Trooper, 1 Parachute Battalion
The beret badge and basic jump-wings are identical except that the former (6a) is surmounted by the national eagle symbol. The old Rhodesian camouflage uniform is still standard issue. (Inset 6b) Cap badge of 1 Commando Battalion.

I1: Australia: Private, 3rd Battalion (Para), Royal Australian Regiment
The RAR badge (1a) is worn on a maroon beret indicating the unit's jump status; personnel not passing a twice-annual fitness test must revert to the dark blue general service beret until they do. The maroon beret was worn by 1 SAS Co. until adopting sand-colour in 1964 on the formation of 1 ASAS Regt.; their badge is inset (1b); 1 Cdo.Regt. wear a distinctive badge on a dark green beret.

I2: People's Republic of China; Fighter, 1st Airborne Division
China's severely plain green uniforms are starting to be replaced in some units by several patterns of camouflage dress. Rank insignia were reinstated in mid-1988, prior to which there had only been two 'rank' categories: 'fighters'—enlisted men, and 'commanders'—officers. The airborne troops adopted a new green service uniform in 1981, including the universal red collar patches and an airborne branch patch (2a) centred on the upper right sleeve.

I3: India; Sergeant, Indian Parachute Regiment
While personnel of other ethnic and religious groups serving in the IPR wear the British-style maroon beret, since 1945 Sikhs have worn a maroon pagri with the same regimental badge (3a); a padded under-helmet is even provided when making a jump. The jump-wings are worn on the right sleeve, and brigade patches on the left, above ranking. The small winged jump indicator badge on the left pocket indicates numbers of jumps completed by the wing colour: blue for 25, yellow for 50, red for 100. In the field a locally-made equivalent of British camouflage uniform is worn.

I4: Indonesia: Korporaal, Para-Commando Regiment, Special Forces Command
The general issue Army badge is worn on a black square plastic backing on a scarlet beret by this unit; airborne infantry and marine paras wear respectively a dark green beret with miniature jump-wings to the right of the badge, and a violet beret. The 'KOMANDO' title (4a) is worn on the right shoulder, the unit patch (4b) on the left, brass jump-wings on the left breast, and light brown-on-OD chevrons on the upper sleeve. (Indonesia has authorised, or tolerated, scores of jump-wing ratings and patterns: one collector estimates that as many as 600 varieties may exist!) Each service's airborne unit wears a different pattern of camouflage uniform.

I5: Japan: Santo Rikuso, 1st Airborne Brigade
Only the Abn.Bde. and Ranger School wear camouflage uniform. Normal jump-wings are similar in shape to the helmet stencil, but ranger-qualified personnel wear the special Ranger wings instead, as here.

I6: South Korea: Captain, 11th Special Forces Brigade
The badge and ranking (6a) are worn on the black beret on a

yellow patch; white diamonds and a black wreath appear as collar ranking in thread on an OD background. Ranger-master parachutist jump-wings are worn in white, with a blue bar backing the wreathed knife indicating ranger qualification, on a camouflage patch on the left breast; it was only in 1981 that a standardised jump-wing design appeared. Each SF Bde. has its own pocket patch.

J1: Malaysia: Private, 21 Para-Commando, Special Services Regiment
The para-commando beret badge is similar to the motif on the unit shoulder patch (1a). Subdued jump-wings are almost universally worn. (Inset 1b) The title and patch of the Ranger Regiment.

J2: New Zealand: Sergeant, 1 New Zealand SAS Squadron
The NZSAS now wear a beret and badge virtually identical to those of their British counterparts, but until 1986 a maroon beret was worn. Field uniforms are devoid of insignia; British-style DPM combat clothing has been introduced. The shoulder title worn in some orders of dress is a shallow arc in maroon with green serif lettering 'NEW ZEALAND SPECIAL/AIR SERVICE'.

J3: Singapore: Lieutenant, 1 Commando Battalion
The badge (3a) worn on the unit's red beret is common throughout Singapore's armed forces. The shoulder patch on the left sleeve (3b) is of recent adoption. Commandos wear jump-wings—here of senior grade—on red backing, instructors on golden yellow. A BDU-pattern camouflage combat uniform

Two *Carabinieri* paratroopers of *1 Battaglione Carabinieri Paracadutisti 'Tuscania'*. The walking-out dress is midnight blue with red piping at collar, shoulder strap and cuff, and above and below the hat band. The silver and red collar patches on white backing are edged red. Note 'Folgore' patch, left sleeve, in yellow and white on blue; red-backed jump-wings; and regimental badge on left breast. The senior NCO wears the two rank bars of Maresciallo Capo, and corresponding slides on the chin strap. (Brian Leigh Davis)

is worn, without insignia.

J4: Sri Lanka: Sergeant-Major, Commando Regiment
The maroon beret bears the badge (4a) common to all army branches, which is embroidered on a patch of the appropriate beret colour; the script reads 'Nothing is Impossible'. The commando qualification badge (4b) is worn beneath the jump-wings. The silver crown of the ranking, which appears on both sleeves, is pinned separately to the embroidered chevrons. The uniform is similar in pattern to US jungle fatigues but of different cut.

J5: Taiwan: Captain, Commando 88
The three bars of rank and infantry rifles are pinned to the collars, and embroidered senior jump-wings are sewn to the left chest. An extremely wide and complex range of SOF unit insignia are used; this officer wears the shoulder title of his unit (5a). (Inset 5b) SF sniper tab. A camouflage uniform similar to S. Korean pattern is also worn.

J6: Thailand: Senior Sergeant, 1st Special Forces Regiment
The maroon beret has now replaced the black previously worn by Thai SF and Rangers, and this camouflage uniform the previously worn 'tiger stripes' with a high percentage of black. Infantry rifles and rank insignia are worn on the collars in black; the Special Warfare Command patch (6b) on the left pocket, by all SF units; and the free-fall qualification tab (6a) on the left shoulder. Senior jump-wings are sewn above the left pocket, in subdued black and blue on OD; Thailand has dozens of different jump-wing ratings and variations, considered by many collectors to be some of the most attractive. (Inset 6c) Patch of 31st Abn.Regt., 1st Infantry Division.

K1: El Salvador: Sargento, 1st Special Operations Group
The 1st SOG and naval infantry wear black berets, but the Abn.Bn. wears none. The 1st SOG wears a US-influenced beret badge and flash (1a) displaying national colours; it also wears a unique shoulder patch and jump-wings. The inset patches are the Abn.Bn. (1b)—its 1st and 2nd Sdns. wear similar patches with gold '1' and '2' on the shroud lines, and 'ESCUADRON' replacing 'BATALLON'. Inset (1c) is the patch of the La Union Naval Inf.Bn.; the Usulatán Bn.'s is similar but with crossed knife (white blade, brown grip) and brown belaying pin.

K2: Guatemala: Sargento Primero, 1st Parachute Battalion of the Army
Besides the battalion shoulder patch, displayed with the 'PARACAIDISTA' and 'KAIBIL' (ranger) titles (2b), the three companies each have their own shoulder patch, plus pocket patches for each of their four platoons; counting the Service Co., the battalion has a total of 20 different patches. This NCO wears the pocket patch of 3rd Plt., 2nd Co., and senior jump-wings. The metal beret badge (2a) follows the design of the battalion patch, and is worn on a red flash—a recent addition, copying that of the US 7th SF Group.

K3: Honduras: Mayor, Special Forces Battalion
Most Honduran units wear olive US-style fatigues, but the SF Bn. wears this 'duck-hunter' camouflage uniform. The 'TESON' (ranger) title (3a) is worn over the US equivalent, earned at Ft. Benning; he also wears the 'Jungle Expert' pocket patch of the US Jungle Operations Course conducted in Panama, and his battalion shoulder patch. Master jump-wings are worn in gilt metal above the rank star on the cap and in yellow thread on the chest. Black-on-OD rank star and infantry rifles are worn on the collars. The flash (inset 3b) is worn on the unit's dark green beret: it is actually the US 5th Inf.Div. patch turned sideways.

K4: Nicaragua: Subteniente, 'Socrates Sandino' Irregular Struggle Battalion
The black beret bears no insignia—indeed, the rank stripe in yellow and red on the shoulder strap is the only embellishment to the uniform. The red and black neckerchief is common among Sandinistas. It is not known if the airborne battalion wears a special beret or insignia.

K5: Cuba: Sargento Segundo, Air Assault and Landing Troops
The camouflage uniform is worn only by SOFs within Cuba, but Cuban expeditionary forces in Africa also use it. The arm-of-service sleeve patch (5a), shoulder board ranking and jump

badge (right breast) are all obviously influenced by Soviet equivalents. (Inset 5b) The arm patch of the naval infantry, who wear Soviet-style black uniforms and berets.

K6: Mexico: Sargento, Parachute Fusilier Brigade
In about 1985 the brigade changed from regular OG fatigues to this special cut, and from violet berets and collar tabs, to the maroon beret (badge, inset 6a) and these collar badges. The left shoulder patch identifies the battalion; the brigade patch (6b) is worn on the right. Ranking is in violet on black slides. Senior jump-wings are worn here.

L1: Argentina: Cabo Primero, 601 Special Forces Group
The uniform has changed little since the Falklands War; the jacket is a local copy of US BDU style, seen here with ranking and jump-wings on the left breast. The Army Commando beret is green; inset are the Army Commando (1a) and Marine Commando (1b) beret badges.

L2: Bolivia: Paracaidista, Parachute Battalion
The beret badge is inset (2a). Ranger battalions wear the same uniform without the beret, but with the ranger badge (2b), which is embroidered and plastic-covered. Several unofficial insignia are also used by the rangers.

L3: Brazil: Cabo, Special Operations Battalion 'Toneleros', Corps of Naval Fusiliers
This old-fashioned looking uniform includes an odd 'Glengarry'-type sidecap; with other uniforms a black beret is worn by these marines. The badge (3a) appears on both types of headgear, and a similar motif in brass as collar badges on this service dress. Naval jump-wings incorporate an anchor behind the parachute. (Inset 3b) Commando patch; (3c) commando qualification badge.

L4: Colombia: Cabo, Battalion of Lancers
The 'LANCERO' badge is awarded in three grades: as worn here, for enlisted men; with a star for assistant instructor NCOs; and with an eagle (4a) for instructor officers. The three-title shoulder patch, for graduates of lancer, parachute and commando courses, is unofficial but tolerated. Note senior grade jump-wings, with star. The red scroll on the cap badge bears 'COMANDOS' in gold.

L5: Ecuador: Sargento, Commando Battalion, Naval Infantry
The navy blue beret has distinctive red rim-piping and a red backing for the badge (5a). The unit's shoulder patch and title, and commando title, are all worn on the left shoulder of service uniforms (5b).

L6: Venezuela: Teniente Primero, Naval Infantry
Officers wear the badge shown on the dark green beret; warrant officers, a somewhat simpler design; and enlisted men the naval infantry badge (6a) on a black triangle, with the national cockade—yellow, blue, red, reading inwards—below it. (Inset 6b) Commando qualification badge. The senior-grade jump-wings are worn on the right breast of the field uniform, which is in US jungle camouflage; a small gilt loop-and-bars rank device is worn on the right collar.

Notes sur les planches en couleur

A1 Les bataillons 2 et 4 de ce régiment, le groupe d'artillerie et la compagnie antiblindés portent ce béret, les bataillons avec écusson (1a). Cartouche (1b) Ecusson de qualification du commando B. **A2** Les hommes des bataillons 1 et 3, l'escadron de reconnaissance et la Compagnie ESR 1 portent ce béret; le bataillon 1 et la Compagnie ESR portent cet écusson et le 3ème bataillon celui présenté en (2a). **A3** Toutes les unités parachutistes métropolitaines portent ce béret rouge et l'écusson TAP depuis septembre 1957. L'écusson régimentaire est porté ici à droite sur la poitrine, et l'insigne de rang sur l'écusson de poitrine. **A4** L'écusson (4a) porté par les unités de parachutistes coloniales/marines en 1958/62 et depuis 1974. Cartouche (4b) Ecusson du centre d'instruction de commando, ici avec un 'R' pour la Réunion. **A5** Le béret et l'écusson proviennent de la formation de cette branche des Chasseurs à pied en 1889. Cartouche (5a) Ecusson, sur la manche gauche, tenue de campagne. **A6** Béret porté sur la droite, et écusson, datant tous deux de la campagne avec les commandos britanniques de la 2ème guerre mondiale. Cartouche (6b) Ecusson de nageur de combat.

B1 Béret et écusson portés par la compagnie 104 de Reconnaissance & de Surveillance et le bataillon de Commando 35. Cartouche (1b) Insigne, sur la manche gauche, tenue de campagne. **B2** Béret et écusson communs à l'ensemble des KNKM; Veste de camouflage britannique portée pendant l'instruction avec les commandos britanniques. Cartouche (2b) Insigne, sur la manche gauche, tenue de campagne. **B3** l'écusson (3a) a des lances; avec une boucle jaune à l'extrémité de la bride d'épaule, c'est la marque de l'héritage que ces unités doivent à la cavalerie. Les écussons de corps d'armée d'épaule sont portés sur le bras gauche de la tenue de campagne—par ex. (3b). Cartouche (3c) Ecusson de corps-à-corps—Einzelkämpferabzeichen. **B4** Bergmütze traditionnel avec écusson d'édelweiss, que ces troupes ont préféré lorsqu'on leur a offert le béret vert en 1971. Cartouche (4a) Ecusson d'épaule de brigade, manche gauche, tenue de campagne; (4b) Ecusson de Chef en montagne. **B5** On ne porte ni béret ni insigne spécial. **B6** Ecusson de béret régimentaire (6a); Le QG de la brigade porte (6b) similaire à l'écusson d'épaule de la Special Service Force. Une feuille blanche sur le brevet de parachutiste indique le service avec une unité de l'armée active aéroportée.

C1 Béret et écussons de col en vert traditionnel des troupes Jaeger. **C2** Seul le personnel de l'école d'instruction des troupes aéroportées porte le béret rouge. **C3** Ecusson de béret (3a), motif traditionnel des Jaeger; insigne sur l'épaule gauche (3b) marque le grade obtenu à l'instruction et se porte sur la tenue de service. **C4** Béret vert porté par les trois régiments, avec écussons régimentaires—ici, I22, écusson comme pièce d'épaule (4a). Les insignes des Régts. K4 et K3 sont présentés respectivement en cartouche (4b) et (4c). Cet uniforme de camouflage expérimental n'a pas été adopté finalement. **C5** L'écusson de l'école de parachutistes se porte sur le béret et sur l'épaule (5a, 5b). **C6** Ecusson avec trident courbé (6a) par les plongeurs d'attaque avec le trident placé à un angle, par le personnel de transport maritime. Cartouche (6b) Insigne de grade et du régiment parent, porté sur la manche.

D1 Ecusson national de béret porté sur le béret rouge des Jaegers. **D2** Béret et écusson (2a) porté par tout le personnel de la Marine; écusson d'épaule des Jaegers de la Marine. **D3** Les unités numérotées portent la version avec matricule de l'écusson, les autres la version (3a). Cartouche (3b) Insigne d'épaule de la brigade depuis 1967. **D4** Les sections parachutistes des brigades alpines et la compagnie deparachutistes du IVè Corps alpin, portent cette coiffure traditionnelle des Alpini. **D5** Béret noir et écusson (5a) datant de 1965; insigne de manchette de l'unité qui ne se porte pas en service actif; insigne national du style de la marine sur la manche. **D6** Ecusson national porté sur le béret vert par les parachutistes, les commandos et cette unité; les marines le portent sur des bérets bleu foncé. Cartouche (6a) Insigne porté sur l'épaule par les unités autres que marines de cette division; (6b) insigne du 32ème Régiment d'Infanterie de Marine.

E1 Insigne de brigade porté sur la manche droite, de bataillon sur la gauche; insigne rouge et or de rang sur le béret et sur la poitrine. Cartouche (1a) Ecusson de béret de parachutistes. **E2** Les distinctions de l'unité sont le béret vert avec écusson (2a), boucle verte sur la patte d'épaule; les écussons de groupements (2b) varient en couleur. **E3** Béret et écusson régimentaires; insigne (3a), sur l'épaule gauche, tenue de service. **E4** Insigne de brigade (4a) porté sur les deux épaules de la tenue de service; béret gris olivâtre et écusson identifiant la brigade. **E5** Pas d'insigne d'unité—écusson de béret porté par tous les éléments de l'armée. **E6** Insigne de rang de style US et brevet de parachutiste (la couronne est retirée) datant du régime du Shah. Cartouche (61) L'une des nombreuses variations d'écusson du béret; (6b) Insigne d'épaule de la tenue de service.

F1 Ecusson national de béret (1a) sur le béret rouge des parachutistes. Ecusson de parachutiste en chute libre sur le côté droit de la poitrine; insigne (1b) sur les deux manches, tenue de service. **F2** Ce bataillon a un béret pourpre royal (avec copie de l'écusson britannique de SAS) et cordon, et écusson spécial de brevet de parachutiste avec couronne et sceptres. Cartouche (2a). Ecusson avec ailes plus simples porté par le Régiment des Parachutistes. **F3** Ecusson national de béret sur le béret rouge; Insigne de Ranger sur la manche au-dessus de l'insigne de rang. **F4** Ecusson national (4a) sur le béret rouge des troupes aéroportées, il semble qu'il soit également porté par certains commandos. Chaque groupe de commando a un écusson (4b) de couleurs différentes. Cartouche (4b, 4c) Ecussons de'épaule de brigade aéroportée et de commando. **F5** Ecusson d'officier (5a) sur le béret bleu des parachutistes; l'écusson de para-commando sur la poitrine marque la qualification de parachutiste et de commando. Cet uniforme de camouflage est spécial aux troupes aéroportées. Cartouche (5b) Ecusson de brigade, tenue de service, épaule gauche; (5c) version en métal de la qualification de para-commando, portée sur la tenue de service. **F6** Insigne de brigade (6a) porté sur la poitrine.

G1 Ecusson de béret national (1a) sur le béret rouge, spécial autrefois aux parachutistes et aux 'forces spéciales' mais, depuis 1985, il est porté par toute l'armée. Ecusson égyptien des parachutistes (voir 3b) sur la poitrine; cartouche (1b), écusson de commando. **G2** Uniforme de style très français, avec écusson de béret de la compagnie (2a) sur le béret rouge et écusson de l'unité sur la poitrine. **G3** Ecusson national de béret (3a); Cartouche (3b) Insigne d'épaule de parachutistes, tenue de service, la version métallique illustrée est quelquefois portée également à gauche sur la poitrine. **G4** Même uniforme que G3, inversé, avec béret noir de commando; cartouche (4a) Insigne d'épaule de commando, porté de la même façon que les parachutistes. **G5** Ecusson de béret (5a) dont le modèle paraît national porté sur le béret bleu des parachutistes. Cartouche (5b) écusson d'épaule, sur les deux manches. **G6** Influence française nette; béret vert porté par tout le personnel militaire avec la tenue de service; la cartouche (6a) est l'écusson de manche gauche de grade et de branche.

H1 Aucun insigne distinctif hormis le brevet de parachutiste. **H2** Cet officier porte la version de l'écusson des troupes; la version correcte des officiers est celle sur (2a); (2b) est l'écusson d'épaule. L'aigle a remplacé le rhinocéros sur l'écusson du béret et le brevet de parachutiste en 1972. **H3** Ecusson de béret (3a) et brevet de parachutiste adopté depuis le retrait des Portugais. **H4** Uniforme de style britannique; camouflage britannique porté sur le terrain. **H5** Ecusson de béret (5a) de parachutistes porté sur le béret rouge; insigne d'épaule de brigade. Cartouche (5b) 2nd bataillon de Parachutistes; (5c) 1er bataillon de parachutistes, il ne fait pas partie de la Brigade 44. **H6** Uniforme de camouflage de la Rhodésie servant toujours, avec écussons de style britannique. Cartouche (6b) Ecusson de béret du Bataillon de Commando 1.

I1 Ecusson régimentaire (1a) porté sur béret rouge par ce bataillon à la formation de parachutistes. Cartouche (1b) Ecusson du Regt 1 ASAS, porté sur béret de couleur sable. **I2** Ecusson des troupes aéroportées (2a) sur la manche droite de la tenue de service. **I3** Les Sikhs ont un pagri rouge foncé spécial avec écusson régimentaire, cartouche (3a); le personnel autre porte un béret rouge foncé. Ecusson avec ailes sur la poitrine indiquant le nombre de sauts—ailes jaunes pour 50 sauts. **I4** Ecusson national sur carré noir sur le béret rouge de ce régiment; cartouches (4a), (4b), insigne sur l'épaule droite et gauche. **I5** Brevet de parachutiste spécial marquant le grade de soldat-Ranger. **I6** L'écusson et l'insigne de grade sur la pièce jaune du béret (6a) diffèrent légèrement de l'insigne de grade sur le col. Chaque brigade a son propre écusson sur la poche gauche; brevet de parachutiste, distinction de maître-Ranger portés ci-dessus.

J1 Ecusson de béret de para-commando et écusson d'épaule semblables (1a). Cartouche (1b) Insige d'épaule de régiment de Ranger. **J2** Depuis 1986 le béret rouge foncé est remplacé par ce style, identique à celui britannique. **J3** Ecusson national (3a) sur le béret rouge de l'unité; écusson d'épaule de l'unité (3b); le fond rouge pour le brevet de parachutiste identifie les commandos. **J4** Ecusson national sur béret rouge foncé de l'unité; écusson de qualification de commando (4b) sous le brevet de parachutiste. **J5** Insignede l'infanterie et grade sur le col; insigne (5a) d'épaule de l'unité. Cartouche (5b) Insigne de tireur d'élite des forces spéciales. **J6** Le béret rouge foncé et la tenue de camouflage ont maintenant remplacé ceux en noir et les 'raies de tigre'. Insigne de grade et d'infanterie sur le col; Ecusson de commandement des Opérations Spéciales sur la poche gauche (6b) par toutes les unités des forces spéciales; qualification de chute libre (6a). Cartouche (6c) 31ème Régt aéroporté, lère Division d'Infanterie.

K1 Ecusson d'unité (1a) sur béret noir, partagé avec l'infanterie de marine; écusson de l'unité et brevet de parachutiste spécial. Cartouche (1b) Bataillon aéroporté; (1c) Bataillon d'infanterie marine La Union. **K2** Ecusson de poche du 3ème peloton, 2ème Compagnie; écusson d'épaule de bataillon; cartouche (2b) insigne d'épaule de parachutiste et de ranger; cartouche (2a) écusson de béret, porté sur un fond rouge. **K3** Insigne 'Teson' sur l'insigne équivalent à celui de Ranger US sur l'épaule, audessus écusson de l'unité; écusson de poche d'expert de la jungle US. Cartouche (3b) Ecusson porté sur le béret vert de l'unité. **K4** Aucun insigne hormis les raies de grade sur les pattes d'épaule; écharpe sandiniste rouge et noire. **K5** L'écusson de manche des troupes aéroportées (5a), l'insigne de grade sur la patte d'épaule et l'écusson de parachutiste sont tous de style soviétique. Cartouche (5b) Ecusson de manche, infanterie de marine. **K6** Uniforme spécial vert foncé et béret rouge foncé (écusson, 6a) datant de 1985 environ. Les écussons de bataillon se portent sur l'épaule gauche, l'écusson de brigade (6b) sur la droite.

L1 Béret et écusson (1a) de commando militaire; insigne de grade à gauche sur la poitrine; cartouche (1b) Ecusson de béret de commando de marine. **L2** Ecusson de béret comme (2a). Les bataillons de Ranger ne portent pas de béret, mais un écusson (2b). **L3** Ecusson de béret (3a) porté également avec la tenue de combat sur le béret noir. Cartouche (3b) Insigne d'unité de commando; (3c) écusson de qualification de commando. **L4** Ecusson de qualification de 'Lancero' porté avec une étoile par les sous-officiers, un aigle par les officiers-instructeurs. Gradation des marques sur l'insigne d'épaule qui sont tolérées mais non officielles, des cours d'instruction de lancier, parachutiste et de commando. **L5** Notez l'écusson et le liseré rourge distinctifs sur le béret bleu marine. Cartouche (5b) écusson d'épaule de l'unité, insigne, et insigne de commando, tenue de service, épaule gauche. **L6** Ecusson de béret des officiers comme ici; les troupes portent (6a) sur un triangle noir avec la cocarde nationale. Notez l'écusson de grade sur le col. Cartouche (6b) écusson de qualification de commando.

Farbtafeln

A1 Das 2. und 4. Bataillon des Regiments, die Artillerieabteilung und die Panzerabwehrkompanie tragen diese Baskenmütze. Die Bataillone besitzen ein Abzeichen. Nebenbild (1b) Commando B Qualifikationsabzeichen. **A2** Das 1. und 3. Bataillon, die Aufklärungsstaffel und die 1. ESR Kompanie tragen diese Baskenmütze; 1. Bataillon und ESR Kompanie haben dieses Abzeichen. Das in Abbildung (2a) gezeigte Abzeichen wird vom 3. Bataillon getragen. **A3** Seit September 1957 ist die rote Baskenmütze mit dem TAP-Abzeichen Bestandteil der Uniform der Fallschirmeinheiten. Das dargestellte Regimentsabzeichen wird auf der rechten Brusthälfte getragen; die Ranginsignie befindet sich am Brustabzeichen. **A4** Das Abzeichen (4a) wurde von den Fallschirmeinheiten der

Marine und den Kolonialstreitkräften zwischen 1958–62 getragen und wurde 1974 wieder eingeführt. Nebenbild (4b) Das Abzeichen des Kommandoausbildungszentrums hat den Buchstaben 'R', der Réunion bedeutet. **A5** Die Baskenm*ütze und das Abzeichen gehen zur Entstehung dieser Truppengattung, die Chasseurs à pied, im Jahre 1889 zurück. Nebenbild (5a) Écusson, linker Ärmel der Dienstuniform. **A6** Eine rechts sitzende Baskenmütze mit Abzeichen der britischen Einheiten im Zweiten Weltkrieg. Nebenbild (6b) Kampfschwimmerabzeichen.

B1 Baskenmütze und Abzeichen der 104. Aufklärungs- und Überwachungskompanie sowie des 35. Kommandobataillons. Nebenbild (1b) Insignie, linker Ärmel der Dienstuniform. **B2** Baskenmütze und Abzeichen, die überall in der KNKM anzufinden waren; Jacke eines Tarnanzugs, der von den britischen Einheiten getragen wurde. Nebenbild (2b) Insignie, linker Ärmel der Dienstuniform. **B3** Das Abzeichen (3a) stellt Lanzen dar. Die gelbe Schlaufe am Schulterstreifen deutet darauf hin, dass die Einheit sich aus der Kavallerie entwickelte. Die Korpsschulterstreifen sind am linken Arm der Dienstuniform, zum Beispiel (3b) zu finden. Nebenbild (3c) Einzelkämpferabzeichen. **B4** Die traditionelle Bergmütze mit Edelweissabzeichen wurde von den Soldaten bevorzugt, als man ihnen im Jahre 1971 die grünen Baskenmützen zur Verfügung stellte. Nebenbild (4a) Brigadeschulterstreifen, linker Ärmel der Dienstuniform; (4b) Bergführer abzeichen. **B5** Keine besondere Baskenmütze oder Insignie wurden getragen. **B6** Regimentsmützen (6a); Uniform der Brigade des Hauptquartiers (6b) mit dem gleichen Schulterstreifen der Special Service Force. Das weisse Blattmuster auf dem Fallschirmflügelabzeichen weist darauf hin, dass es sich um eine aktive Einheit handelt.

C1 Abzeichen am Kragen und der Baskenmütze sind im althergebrachten grün der Jaeger Soldaten gehalten. **C2** Nur das fliegende Ausbildungspersonal besitzt eine rote Baskenmütze. **C3** Das Baskenmützenabzeichen (3a) mit dem üblichen Jaeger-Motiv; linke Schulterinsignie (3b) deutet auf die Absolvierung des Lehrgangs hin und wurde auf der Dienstuniform angebracht. **C4** Die drei Regimenter trugen alle grüne Baskenmützen mit Regimentsabzeichen. Zu sehen ist hier I22; das Abzeichen wird als Schulterabzeichen getragen (4a). Die Insignien her Regimenter K4 und K3 sind in (4b) und (4c) entsprechend abgebildet. Diese experimentelle Tarnuniform wurde letztendlich nicht übernommen. **C5** Das Abzeichen der Fallschirmspringerscule fand sich auf der Baskenmütze und der Schulter wieder (5a, 5b). **C6** Abzeichen mit gebogenem Dreizack (6a), der von den Angriffstauchern getragen wurde; das Schiffstransportpersonal trägt den angewinkelten Dreizack. Nebenbild (6b) Ärmelinsignie des Regiments und für den Lehrgangsabschluss.

D1 Nationales Mützenabzeichen (1a) auf der roten Baskenmütze der Jaeger. **D2** Baskenmütze und Abzeichen des gesamten Marinepersonals; Schulterabzeichen der Marine-Jaeger. **D3** Die numerierten Einheiten tragen numerierte Abzeichen, die anderen die Version in (3a). Nebenbild (3b) Schulterinsignie der Brigade seit dem Jahr 1967. **D4** Fallschirmspringerzug der Alpenbrigade und Fallschirmspringerkompanie des IV. Alpenkorps. Alle Einheiten tragen die übliche Mütze der Alpini. **D5** Eine schwarze Baskenmütze mit Abzeichen (5a) aus dem Jahre 1965. Die Manschetteninsignie der Einheit wurden im Einsatz nicht getragen. Die nationale Ärmelinsignie folgt dem Marinemuster. **D6** Nationales Abzeichen auf dem grünen Baskenmützen der Fallschirmspringer, Kommandoeinheiten und diese Einheit; die Seesoldaten tragen am dunkelblauen Baskenmützen. Nebenbild (6a) Schulterinsignie landgestützer Einheiten der Division; (6b) Insignie des 32. Marineinfanterieregiments.

E1 Brigadeinsignie am rechten Ärmel, Batailloninsignie links; die rote und goldene Ranginsignie ist an der Brust und den Baskenmützen zu erkennen. Nebenbild (1a) Baskenmützenabzeichen der Fallschirmspringer. **E2** Einheitsauszeichnungen setzen sich aus einer grünen Baskenmütze mit Abzeichen (2a) und grüner Schlaufe am Schulterstreifen zusammen; Gruppenabzeichen (2b) unterscheiden sich durch Farben. **E3** Regimentsbaskenmütze und –abzeichen; Insignie (3a) an der linken Schulter der Dienstuniform. **E4** Die Brigadeinsignie (4a) auf beiden Schultern der Dienstuniform. Eintönige olivgrüne Baskenmützen und Abzeichen der Brigade. **E5** Keine Einheitsinsignie—Mützenabzeichen der gesamten Armee. **E6** Ranginsignien—die dem US-amerikanischen Stil folgen—sowie Flügelabzeichen (ohne Krone) der Fallschirmspringer aus der Zeit des Schahs. Nebenbild (6a) Eine der vielen Mützenabzeichenvariationen; (6b) Schulterinsignie der Dienstuniform.

F1 Nationales Mützenabzeichen (1a) auf der roten Baskenmütze des Fallschirmspringers. Abzeichen des freifallenden Fallschirmspringers auf der rechten Brusthälfte. Die Insignie (1b) befindet sich auf beiden Ärmeln der Dienstuniform. **F2** Dieses Bataillon besitzt die königliche purpurfarbene Baskenmütze (mit einer Nachbildung des britischen SAS-Abzeichens), Kordel und einem besonderen Fallschirmspringerflügelabzeichen mit Krone und Zeptern. Nebenbild (2a) Wenig dekoriertes Flügelabzeichen des Fallschirmspringerregiments. **F3** Nationales Mützenabzeichen (4a) auf roter Baskenmütze; Ranger-Insignie am Ärmel über der Ranginsignie. **F4** Nationales Abzeichen (4a) auf der roten Baskenmütze der fliegenden Soldaten. Es wurde angeblich auch von anderen Kommandos verwendet. Jede Kommandogruppe besitzt ein verschiedenfarbiges Abzeichen (4b). Nebenbild (4b, 4c) Schulterabzeichen der Luft- und Kommandobrigade. **F5** Offiziersabzeichen (5a) auf blauer Baskenmütze der Fallschirmspringer. Brustabzeichen der Fallschirmspringerkommandos dient zur Qualifizierung der Fallschirmjäger und des Kommandos. Diese Tarnuniform wird nur von den fliegenden Soldaten getragen. Nebenbild (5b) Brigadeabzeichen auf der linken Schulter der Dienstuniform. (5c) Eine metallen Version der Qualifikation an der Dienstuniform des Luftlandekommandos. **F6** Brigadeinsignie (6a) an der Brust.

G1 Nationales Mützenabzeichen (1a) auf roter Baskenmütze wurde einst nur von den Fallschirmspringern und 'Spezialeinheiten' getragen, aber ist seit 1985 überall in der Armee zu finden. Brustabzeichen der ägyptischen Fallschirmspringer (siehe 3b). Nebenbild (1b) Kommandoabzeichen. **G2** Eine äusserst

französische anmutende Uniform mit Mützenabzeichen der Kompanie (2a) auf roter Baskenmütze und Brustabzeichen. **G3** Nationales Mützenabzeichen (3a); Nebenbild (3b) Schulterinsignie der Fallschirmspringer an der Dienstuniform. Das abgebildete Metallabzeichen wurde manchmal auch der linken Brusthälfte getragen. **G4** Schulterinsignie des Kommandos, welches genauso getragen wie das der Fallschirmspringer. **G5** Mützenabzeichen (5a). Anscheinend ein einheimischer Entwurf, der von den Fallschirmspringern auf der Baskenmütze getragen wird. Nebenbild (5b) Schulterinsignie an beiden Ärmeln. **G6** Der französische Einfluss ist nicht zu verleugnen; eine grüne Maskenmütze die Bestandteil der Dienstuniform aller Armeeverbände ist. Nebenbild (6a) Linker Ärmel mit Rang- und Abteilungs-Écusson.

H1 Ausser dem Flügelabzeichen der Fallschirmspringer war dies keine auffallende Insignie. **H2** Dieser Offizier trägt das Abzeichen der Soldaten, das richtige Offizierabzeichen ist in (2a) abgebildet. (2b) Schulterstreifen. Das Nashorn wurde durch den Adler aus Mützenabzeichen und dem Flügelabzeichen der Fallschirmspringer im Jahr 1972 ausgetauscht. **H3** Baskenmützenabzeichen (3a) und Flügelabzeichen der Fallschirmspringer wurde seitdem Abzug der portugiesischen Einheit übernommen. **H4** Eine dem britische Stil entsprechende Uniform; britische Tarnbekleidung für den Kampfeinsatz. **H5** Abzeichen (5a) auf der roten Baskenmütze der Fallschirmspringer. Schulterinsignie der Brigade. Nebenbild (5b) 2. Fallschirmspringer Bataillon, (5c) 1. Fallschirmspringer Bataillon, welches nicht der 44. Brigade angehört. **H6** Die noch im Gebrauch befindlichen Tarnanzüge in Rhodesien mit den im britischen Stil gehaltenen Abzeichen. Nebenbild (6b) Abzeichen des 1. Kommandobataillons.

I1 Regimentsabzeichen (1a) auf roter Baskenmütze, welches vom im Fallschirmspringen ausgebildeten Bataillon getragen wurde. Nebenbild (1b) 1. ASAS Regimentsabzeichen, welches auf einer sandfarbenen Baskenmütze getragen wird. **I2** Rechtes Ärmelabzeichen (2a) der Dienstuniform des fliegenden Personals. **I3** Sikhs haben einen besonderen kastanienbraunen Pagri mit Regimentsabzeichen, Nebenbild (3b); das restliche Dienstpersonal trägt kastanienbraune Baskenmützen. Die Flügelabzeichen geben Aufschluss über die Zahl der Absprünge—das gelbe Flügelabzeichen entspricht 50 Absprüngen. **I4** Nationales Abzeichen auf scharzem Quadrat wird an der roten Baskenmütze dieses Regiments getragen. Nebenbild (4a), (4b), rechte und linke Schulterinsignie. **I5** Besonderes Flügelabzeichen der Fallschirmspringer, die als qualifizierte Ranger-Salden ausgezeichnet sind. **I6** Abzeichen- und Ranginsignie auf dem Baskensmützenstreifen (6a) unterscheidet sich etwas von der Ranginsignie am Kragen. Jede Brigade hat einen anderen linken Taschenstreifen. Oben sind die Flügelabzeichen des obersten Ranger-Fallschirmspringers abgebildet.

J1 Baskenmützeninsignie des Fallschirmspringerkommandos und Schulterstreifen sind ähnlich (1a). Nebenbild (1b) Schulterinsignie des Ranger-Regiments. **J2** Die kastanienfarbene Baskenmütze ist seit 1986 mit dieser Mütze ausgetauscht worden; die andere im britischen Stil gehalten. **J3** Nationales Abzeichen (3a) auf roter Baskenmütze der Einheit; Schulterstreifen der Einheit (3b); der rote Hintergrund deutet auf das Kommando hin. **J4** Nationales Abzeichen auf den kastanienfarbenen Baskenmützen der Einheit. Qualifikationsabzeichen des Kommandos (4b) befindet sich unter dem Flügelabzeichen der Fallschirmspringer. **J5** Insignie der Infanterie und des Ranges am Kragen; Schulterinsignie der Einheit (5a). Nebenbild (5b) Heckenschützen-Insignie der Spezialeinheit. **J6** Die ehemalige schwarze Dienstuniform mit 'Tigerstreifen' wurde mit Tarnanzügen und kastanienfarbener Baskenmütze ausgewechselt. Rang- und Infanterieinsignie werden am Kragen; zum an der linken Tasche ist der Streifen des Spezialkommandos für die Kriegsführung zu erkennen (6b) und wird von allen Spezialeinheiten und dazugehörigen Einheiten verwendet. (6a) Qualifikationsabzeichen für den freien Fall. Nebenbild (6c) 31. Fliegerregiment, 1. Infanteriedivision.

K1 Einheitsabzeichen (1a) auf schwarzer Baskenmütze wurde auch von Marineinfanteristen getragen; Einheitsstreifen und Flügelabzeichen der Sonderluftlandetruppen. Nebenbild (1b) Fliegerbataillon, (1c) La Union Naval Infanteriebataillon. **K2** Taschenabzeichen des 3. Zugs, 2. Kompanie; Schulterstreifen des Bataillons; Nebenbild (2b) Schulterinsignie der Fallschirmjäger und Ranger. Nebenbild (2a) Mützenabzeichen mit rotem Hintergrund getragen. **K3** 'Treson'-Insignie über den gleichen US-'Ranger'-Insignie an der Schulter; oben Einheitsstreifen. Taschenabzeichen des US-Dschungelexperten. Nebenbild (3b) Streifen, die auf der grünen Baskenmütze der Einheit getragen wird. **K4** Ausser den Rangstreifen am Schulterstreifen keine Insignie; rotschwarzer Schal der Sandinista. **K5** Ärmelabzeichen der fliegenden Sodaten (5a). Ranginsignie am Schulterstreifen sowie Fallschirmspringerabzeichen sind im sowjetischen Stil gehalten. Nebenbild (5b) Ärmelabzeichen der Marineinfanterie. **K6** Dunkelgrüne Spezialuniform und kastianienfarbene Baskenmütze (Azeichen 6a) datieren cirka aus dem Jahr 1985. Bataillonsabzeichen auf der linken Schulter und Brigadeabzeichen rechts (6b).

L1 Baskenmütze des Heereskommandos mit Abzeichen (1a); Ranginsignie au der linken Brusthälfte. Nebenbild (1b) Mützenabzeichen des Marinekommandos. **L2** Baskenmützenabzeichen wie (2a). Ranger-Bataillone tragen eine Baskenmützen, aber ein Tuchabzeichen (2b). **L3** Mützenabzeichen (3a) wird auch mit Kampfanzug und schwarzer Baskenmütze getragen. Nebenbild (3b Einheitsinsignie des Kommandos; (3c) Qualifizierungsabzeichen des Kommandos. **L4** 'Lanzero'-Qualifikationsabzeichen, welches mit einem Stern der Unteroffizier getragen wird, wohingegen der Offiziersausbilder einen Adler ha (4a). Zugelassene aber inoffizielle Schulterinsignie nachdem der Lehrgang deleichten Panzerverbände oder Fallschirmspringer absolviert ist. **L5** Auffallend ist das rote Tuchzeichen und Paspel an der blauen Baskenmütze der marine Nebenbild (5b) Schulterabzeichen der Einheit, Orden und Kommandoinsignie am linken Ärmel der Dienstuniform. **L6** Hier Mützenabzeichen des Offizier Soldaten tragen (6a) auf schwarzem Hintergrund mit Nationalkokarde. Z bemerken ist das Kragenabzeichen. Nebenbild (6b) Qualifikationsabzeichen de Kommandos.